COVER ILLUSTRATIONS

Front cover: Grand Teton and Lake Solitude, back country, Grand Teton National Park. **Photo by Glenn Van Nimwegen, Jackson, Wyoming.**

Inside front cover: View west up Cascade Canyon, with north face of Mt. Owen in center. **National Park Service photo by H. D. Pownall.**

Back cover: Grand Teton, Mt. Owen, and Mt. Teewinot from Jenny Lake Flat. **National Park Service photo by W. E. Dilley.**

Inside back cover: View southwest from Lake Solitude toward the Grand Teton (right), Mt. Owen, and Mt. Teewinot. **Wyoming Travel Commission photo by J. R. Simon.**

Inside fold: Geologic Map of Grand Teton National Park.

To Fritiof M. Fryxell, geologist, teacher, writer, mountaineer, and the first ranger-naturalist in Grand Teton National Park. All who love and strive to understand the Teton landscape follow in his footsteps.

Creative Director:	Century III Advertising, Inc.
Designer:	Les Hays Studios, Inc.
Color Separations –	
Assembly – Plates:	Orent Graphic Arts, Inc.
Type:	Bodoni and Gothic
Printer:	Omaha Printing Co.
Printing:	Offset Lithography. Six Colors on Covers Two Colors on Body

CREATION OF THE TETON LANDSCAPE

The Geologic Story of Grand Teton National Park

By

J. D. LOVE AND JOHN C. REED, JR.
U.S. Geological Survey

Library of Congress Catalog Card No.: 68-20628

Reprinted 1995

Grand Teton Natural History Association
Moose, Wyoming 83012

CONTENTS

Foreword 6

THE STORY BEGINS 8
First questions, brief answers 9
An extraordinary story 10
An astronaut's view 12
A pilot's view 14
A motorist's view 15
 View north 15
 View west 18
 View south 19
A mountaineer's view 20

CARVING THE RUGGED PEAKS 24
Steep mountain slopes—the perpetual battleground 24
Rock disintegration and gravitational movement 24
Running water cuts and carries 26
Glaciers scour and transport 28
Effects on Jackson Hole 30

MOUNTAIN UPLIFT 36
Kinds of mountains 36
Anatomy of faults 38
Time and rate of uplift 40
Why are mountains here? 41
The restless land 43

ENORMOUS TIME AND DYNAMIC EARTH 45
Framework of time 45
Rocks and relative age 45
Fossils and geologic time 46
Radioactive clocks 47
The yardstick of geologic time 48

**PRECAMBRIAN ROCKS—THE CORE OF
THE TETONS** 51
Ancient gneisses and schists 51
Granite and pegmatite 55

Black dikes 58

Quartzite 63

A backward glance 64

The close of the Precambrian—end of the beginning 64

THE PALEOZOIC ERA—TIME OF LONG-VANISHED SEAS AND THE DEVELOPMENT OF LIFE 66

The Paleozoic sequence 66

Alaska Basin—site of an outstanding rock
and fossil record 66

Advance and retreat of Cambrian seas; an example 69

Younger Paleozoic formations 74

THE MESOZOIC—ERA OF TRANSITION 79

Colorful first Mesozoic strata 79

Drab Cretaceous strata 81

Birth of the Rocky Mountains 82

TERTIARY—TIME OF MAMMALS, MOUNTAINS, LAKES, AND VOLCANOES 86

Rise and burial of mountains 88

The first big lake 92

Development of mammals 95

Volcanoes 98

QUATERNARY—TIME OF ICE, MORE LAKES, AND CONTINUED CRUSTAL DISTURBANCE ...102

Hoback normal fault 103

Volcanic activity 103

Preglacial lakes 104

The Ice Age 105

Modern glaciers 112

THE PRESENT AND THE FUTURE 113

APPENDIX 115

Acknowledgements 115

Selected references—if you wish to read further 116

About the authors 117

Index of selected terms and features 118

FOREWORD

Geology is the science of the Earth — the study of the forces, processes, and past life that not only shape our land but influence our daily lives and our Nation's welfare. This booklet, prepared by two members of the U.S. Geological Survey, discusses how geologic phenomena are responsible for the magnificent scenery of the Teton region.

Recognition of the complex geologic history of our Earth is vital to the enjoyment and appreciation of beautiful landscapes and other natural wonders, to the planning of our cities and highway systems, to the wise use of our water supplies, to the study of earthquake and landslide areas, to the never-ending search for new mineral deposits, and to the conservation and development of our known natural resources. Who can say, in the long run, which of the many uses of this knowledge is the most compelling reason to seek an understanding of the Earth?

W. T. Pecora, *Director*
U.S. Geological Survey

This booklet is based on geologic investigations by the U. S. Geological Survey in cooperation with the National Park Service, U. S. Department of Interior.

"Something hidden. Go and find it.
Go and look behind the Ranges--
Something lost behind the Ranges.
Lost and waiting for you. Go."

KIPLING — *THE EXPLORER*

THE TETON RANGE is one of the most magnificent mountain ranges on the North American Continent. Others are longer, wider, and higher, but few can rival the breathtaking alpine grandeur of the eastern front of the Tetons. Ridge after jagged ridge of naked rock soar upward into the western sky, culminating in the towering cluster of peaks to which the early French voyageurs gave the name *"les Trois Tetons"* (the three breasts). The range hangs like a great stone wave poised to break across the valley at its base. To the south and east are lesser mountains, interesting and scenic but lacking the magic appeal of the Tetons.

This is a range of many moods and colors: stark and austere in morning sun, but gold and purple and black in the softly lengthening shadows of afternoon; somber and foreboding when the peaks wrap themselves in the tattered clouds of an approaching storm, but tranquil and ethereal blue and silver beneath a full moon.

These great peaks and much of the floor of the valley to the east, *Jackson Hole* (a *hole* was the term used by pioneer explorers and mountain men to describe any open valley encircled by mountains), lie within Grand Teton National Park, protected and preserved for the enjoyment of present and future generations. Each year more than 3 million visitors come to the park. Many pause briefly and pass on. Others stay to explore its trails, fish its streams, study the plants and wildlife that abound within its borders, or to savor the colorful human history of this area.

Most visitors, whatever their interests and activities, are probably first attracted to the park by its unsurpassed mountain scenery. The jagged panorama of the Tetons is the backdrop to which they may turn again and again, asking questions, seeking answers. How did the mountains form? How long have they towered into the clouds, washed by rain, riven by frost, swept by wind and snow? What enormous forces brought them forth and raised them skyward? What stories are chronicled in their rocks, what epics chiseled in the craggy visage of this mountain landscape? Why are the Tetons different from other mountains?

First questions, brief answers

How did the Tetons and Jackson Hole form? They are both tilted blocks of the earth's crust that behaved like two adjoining giant trapdoors hinged so that they would swing in opposite directions. The block on the west, which forms the Teton Range, was hinged along the Idaho-Wyoming State line; the eastern edge was uplifted along a *fault* (a fracture along which displacement has occurred). This is why the highest peaks and steepest faces are near the east margin of the range. The hinge line of the eastern block, which forms Jackson Hole, was in the highlands to the east. The western edge of the block is downdropped along the fault at the base of the Teton Range. As a consequence, the floor of Jackson Hole tilts westward toward the Tetons (see cross section inside back cover).

When did the Tetons and Jackson Hole develop the spectacular scenery we see today? The Tetons are the youngest of all the mountain ranges in the Rocky Mountain chain. Most other mountains in the region are at least 50 million years old but the Tetons are less than 10 million and are still rising. Jackson Hole is of the same age and is still sinking. The Teton landscape is the product of many earth processes, the most recent of which is cutting by water and ice. Within the last 15,000 years, ice sculpturing of peaks and canyons and impounding of glacial lakes have added finishing touches to the scenic beauty.

Why did the Tetons rise and Jackson Hole sink? For thousands of years men have wondered about the origin of mountains and their speculations have filled many books. Two of the more popular theories are: (1) continental drift (such as South America moving away from Africa), with the upper lighter layer of the earth's crust moving over the lower denser layer and wrinkling along belts of weakness; and (2) convection currents within the earth, caused by heat transfer, resulting in linear zones of wrinkling, uplift, and collapse.

These concepts were developed to explain the origin of mountainous areas hundreds or thousands of miles long but they do not answer directly the question of why the Tetons rose and Jackson Hole sank. As is discussed in the chapter on mountains, it is probable that semifluid rock far below the surface of Jackson Hole flowed north into the Yellowstone Volcanic Plateau-Absaroka Range volcanic area, perhaps taking the place of the enormous amount of ash and lava blown out of volcanoes during the last 50 million years. The origin of the line of weakness that marks the Teton fault along the east face of the Teton Range may go back to some unknown inequality in the earth's composition several billion years ago. Why it suddenly became active late in the earth's history is an unanswered question.

The ultimate source of heat and energy that caused the mountains and basins to form probably is disintegration of radioactive materials deep within the earth. The Tetons are a spectacular demonstration that the enormous energy necessary to create mountains is not declining, even though our planet is several billion years old.

An extraordinary story

Visitors whose curiosity is whetted by this unusual and varied panorama are not satisfied with only a few questions and answers. They sense that here for the asking is an extraordinary *geologic* (*geo*—earth; *logic*—science) story. With a little direction, many subtle features become evident —features that otherwise might escape notice. Here, for example, is a valley with an odd U-shape. There is a sheer face crisscrossed with light- and dark-colored rocks. On the valley floor is a tuft of pine trees that seem to be confined to one particular kind of rock. On the rolling hills is a layer of peculiar white soil—the only soil in which coyote dens are common. All these are geologically controlled phenomena. In short, with a bit of initial guidance, the viewer gains an ability to observe and to understand so much that the panorama takes on new depth, vividness, and excitement. It changes from a flat, two-dimensional picture to a colorful multi-dimensional exhibit of the earth's history.

10

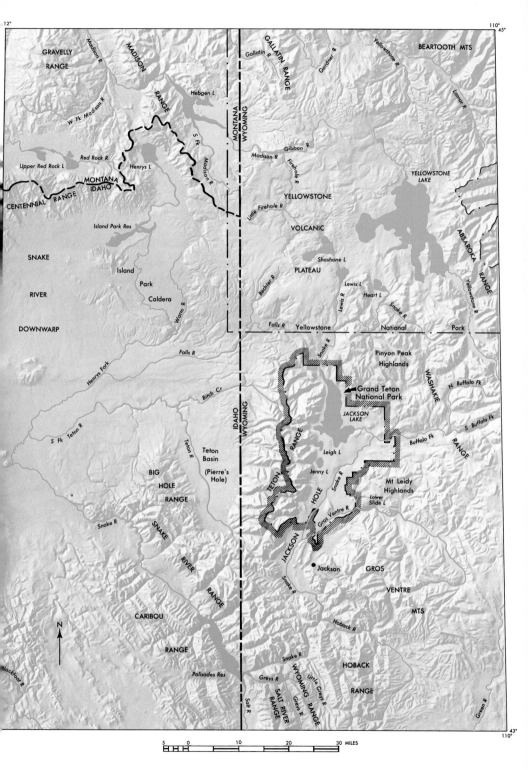

Figure 1. *The Tetons from afar—an astronaut's view of the range and adjacent mountains, basins, and plateaus. Width of area shown in photo is about 100 miles. Stippled pattern marks boundary of Grand Teton National Park.*

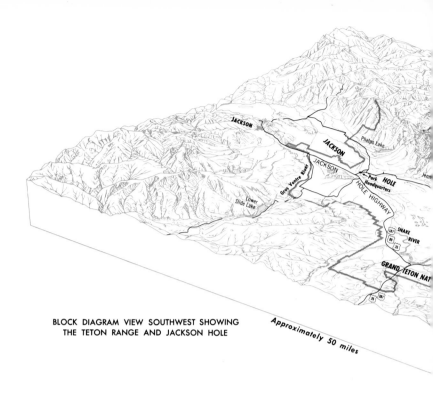

BLOCK DIAGRAM VIEW SOUTHWEST SHOWING
THE TETON RANGE AND JACKSON HOLE

Approximately 50 miles

An astronaut's view

The Tetons are a short, narrow, and high mountain range, distinctive in the midst of the great chain of the Rocky Mountains, the backbone of western North America. Figure 1 shows how the Tetons and their surroundings might appear if you viewed them from a satellite at an altitude of perhaps a hundred miles. The U. S. Geological Survey topographic map of Grand Teton National Park shows the names of many features not indicated on figure 1 or on the geologic map inside the back cover. The Teton Range is a rectangular mountain block about 40 miles long and 10-15 miles wide. It is flanked on the east and west by flat-floored valleys. Jackson Hole is the eastern one and Teton Basin (called Pierre's Hole by the early trappers) is the western.

The Teton Range is not symmetrical. The highest peaks lie near the eastern edge of the mountain block, rather than along its center, as is true in conventional mountains, and the western slopes are broad and gentle in

12

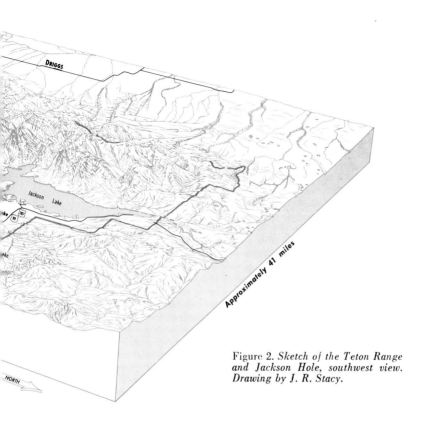

Figure 2. *Sketch of the Teton Range and Jackson Hole, southwest view. Drawing by J. R. Stacy.*

contrast to the precipitous eastern slopes. The northern end of the range disappears under enormous lava flows that form the Yellowstone Volcanic Plateau. Even from this altitude the outlines of some of these flows can be seen.

On the south the Teton Range abuts almost at right angles against a northwest-trending area of lower and less rugged mountains (the Snake River, Wyoming, and Hoback Ranges). These mountains appear altogether different from the Tetons. They consist of a series of long parallel ridges cut or separated by valleys and canyons. This pattern is characteristic of mountains composed of crumpled, steeply tilted rock layers—erosion wears away the softer layers, leaving the harder ones standing as ridges.

On the east and northeast, Jackson Hole is bounded by the Gros Ventre and Washakie Ranges, which are composed chiefly of folded hard and soft sedimentary rocks. In con-

13

trast, between these mountains and the deepest part of Jackson Hole to the west, thick layers of soft nearly flat-lying sedimentary rocks have been sculptured by streams and ice into randomly oriented knife-edge ridges and rolling hills separated by broad valleys. The hills east of the park are called the Mount Leidy Highlands and those northeast are the Pinyon Peak Highlands.

A pilot's view

If you descend from 100 miles to about 5 miles above the Teton region, the asymmetry of the range, the extraordinary variety of landscapes, and the vivid colors of rocks become more pronounced.

Figure 2 shows a panorama of the Teton Range and Jackson Hole from a vantage point over the Pinyon Peak Highlands. The rough steep slopes and jagged ridges along the east front of the range contrast with smoother slopes and more rounded ridges on the western side. Nestled at the foot of the mountains and extending out onto the floor of Jackson Hole are tree-rimmed sparkling lakes of many sizes and shapes. Still others lie in steep-sided rocky amphitheaters near the mountain crests.

One of the most colorful flight routes into Jackson Hole is from the east, along the north flank of the Gros Ventre Mountains. For 40 miles this mountain range is bounded by broad parallel stripes of bright-red, pink, purple, gray, and brown rocks. Some crop out as cliffs or ridges, and others are *badlands* (bare unvegetated hills and valleys with steep slopes and abundant dry stream channels). In places the soft beds have broken loose and flowed down slopes like giant varicolored masses of taffy. These are mudflows and landslides. The colorful rocks are bounded on the south by gray and yellow tilted layers forming snowcapped peaks of the Gros Ventre Mountains.

These landscapes are the product of many natural forces acting on a variety of rock types during long or short intervals of geologic time. Each group of rocks records a chapter in the geologic story of the region. Other chapters can be read from the tilting, folding, and breaking of the rocks. The latest episodes are written on the face of the land itself.

14

Most park visitors first see the Teton peaks from the highway. Whether they drive in from the south, east, or north, there is one point on the route at which a spectacular panorama of the Tetons and Jackson Hole suddenly appears. Part of the thrill of these three views is that they are so unexpected and so different. The geologic history is responsible for these differences.

View north.—Throughout the first 4 miles north of the town of Jackson, the view of the Tetons from U. S. 26-89 is blocked by East Gros Ventre Butte. At the north end of the butte, the highway climbs onto a flat upland at the south boundary of Grand Teton National Park. Without any advance warning, the motorist sees the whole east front of the Teton Range rising steeply from the amazingly flat floor of Jackson Hole.

From the park boundary turnout no lakes or rivers are visible to the north but the nearest line of trees in the direction of the highest Teton peaks marks the approximate position of the Gros Ventre River. The elevation of this river is surprising, for the route has just come up a 150-foot hill, out of the flat valley of a much smaller stream, yet here at eye-level is a major river perched on an upland plain. The reason for these strange relations is that the hill is a fault scarp (see fig. 16A for a diagram) and the valley in which the town of Jackson is located was dropped 150 feet or more in the last 15,000 years.

On the skyline directly west of the turnout are horizontal and inclined layers of rocks. These once extended over the tops of the highest peaks but were worn away from some parts as the mountains rose. All along the range, trees grow only up to *treeline* (also called *timberline*—a general elevation above which trees do not grow) which here is about 10,500 feet above the sea. To the southeast and east, beyond the sage-covered floor of Jackson Hole, are rolling partly forested slopes marking the west end of the Gros Ventre Mountains. They do not look at all like the Tetons because they were formed in a very different manner. The Gros Ventres are folded mountains that have foothills; the Tetons are faulted mountains that do not.

15

Figure 3A. *The Teton landscape as seen from Signal Mountain. View west acros.*

Figure 3B. *The Teton landscape as seen from Signal Mountain*

16

...ackson Lake. Major peaks, canyons, and outcrops of sedimentary rocks are indicated by **"s."**

...iew northeast; a study in contrast with the panorama above.

17

Three steepsided hills called *buttes* rise out of the flat floor of Jackson Hole. They are tilted and faulted masses of hard, layered rock that have been shaped by southward-moving glaciers. Six miles north of the boundary turnout is Blacktail Butte, on the flanks of which are west-dipping white beds. Southwest of the turnout is East Gros Ventre Butte, composed largely of layered rocks that are exposed along the road from Jackson almost to the turnout. These are capped by very young lava that forms the brown cliff overlooking the highway at the north end of the butte. To the southwest is West Gros Ventre Butte, composed of similar rocks.

View west.—The motorist traveling west along U. S. 26-287 is treated to two magnificent views of the Teton Range. The first is 8 miles and the second 13 miles west of Togwotee Pass. At these vantage points, between 20 and 30 miles from the mountains, the great peaks seem half suspended between earth and sky—too close, almost, to believe, but too distant to comprehend.

Only from closer range can the motorist begin to appreciate the size and steepness of the mountains and to discern the details of their architecture. The many roads on the floor of Jackson Hole furnish ever-changing vistas, and signs provided by the National Park Service at numerous turnouts and scenic overlooks help the visitor to identify quickly the major peaks and canyons and the principal features of the valley floor. Of all these roadside vantage points, the top of Signal Mountain, an isolated hill rising nearly 1,000 feet out of the east margin of Jackson Lake, probably offers the best overall perspective (fig. 3). To the west, across the shimmering blue waters of Jackson Lake, the whole long parade of rugged peaks stretches from the north horizon to the south, many of the higher ones wearing the tattered remnants of winter snow. From here, only 8 miles away, the towering pinnacles, saw-toothed ridges, and deep U-shaped canyons are clearly visible.

Unlike most other great mountain ranges, the Tetons rise steeply from the flat valley floor in a straight unbroken line. The high central peaks tower more than a mile above the valley, but northward and southward the peaks diminish in height and lose their jagged character, gradually giving way to lower ridges and rounded hills. Some of the details of the mountain rock can be seen—gnarled gray rocks of the high peaks threaded by a fine white lacework of dikes, the dark band that cleaves through Mount Moran from base to summit, and the light brown and gray layers on the northern and southern parts of the range.

At first glance the floor of Jackson Hole south of Signal Mountain seems flat, smooth, and featureless, except for the Snake River that cuts diagonally across it. Nevertheless, even the flats show a variety of land forms. The broad sage-covered areas, low isolated hills, and hummocky tree-studded ridges that form the foreground are all parts of the Teton landscape, and give us clues to the natural processes that shaped it. A critical look to the south discloses more strange things. We take for granted the fact that the sides of normal valleys slope inward toward a central major stream. South of Signal Mountain, however, the visitor can see that the Snake River Valley does not fit this description. The broad flat west of the river should slope east but it does not. Instead, it has been tilted westward by downward movement along the Teton fault at the base of the mountains.

View south.—About a million motorists drive south from Yellowstone to Grand Teton National Park each year. As they wind along the crooked highway on the west brink of Lewis River Canyon (fig. 1), the view south is everywhere blocked by dense forest. Then, abruptly the road leaves the canyon, straightens out, and one can look south down a 3-mile sloping avenue cut through the trees. There, 20 to 30 miles away, framed by the roadway, are the snow-capped Tetons, with Jackson Lake, luminous in reflected light, nestled against the east face. This is one of the loveliest and most unusual views of the mountains that is available to the motorist, partly because he is 800 feet above the level of Jackson Lake and partly because this is the only place on a main highway where he can see clearly the third dimension (width) of the Tetons. The high peaks are on the east edge; they rise 7,000 feet above the lake but other peaks and precipitous ridges, progressively diminishing in

19

height, extend on to the west for a dozen miles (fig. 14). Giant, relatively young lava flows, into which the Lewis River Canyon was cut, poured southward all the way to the shore of Jackson Lake and buried the north end of the Teton Range (figs. 13 and 53). South of Yellowstone Park these flows were later tilted and broken by the dropping of Jackson Hole and the rise of the mountains.

A mountaineer's view

As in many pursuits in life, the greatest rewards of a visit to the Tetons come to those who expend a real effort to earn them. Only by leaving the teeming valley and going up into the mountains to hike the trails and climb the peaks can the visitor come to know the Tetons in all their moods and changes and view close at hand the details of this magnificent mountain edifice.

Even a short hike to Hidden Falls and Inspiration Point affords an opportunity for a more intimate view of the mountains. Along the trail the hiker can examine outcrops of sugary white granite, glittering mica-studded dikes, and dark intricately layered rocks. Nearby are great piles of broken fragments that have fallen from the cliffs above, and the visitor can begin to appreciate how vulnerable are the towering crags to the relentless onslaught of frost and snow. The roar of the foaming stream and the thunder of the falls are constant reminders of the patient work of running water in wearing away the "everlasting hills." Running his hand across one of the smoothly polished rock faces below Inspiration Point, the hiker gains an unforgettable concept of the power of glacial ice and its importance in shaping this majestic landscape. Looking back across Jenny Lake at the encircling ridge of glacial debris, he can easily comprehend the size of the ancient glacier that once flowed down Cascade Canyon and emerged onto the floor of Jackson Hole.

The more ambitious hiker or mountaineer can seek out the inner recesses of the range and explore other facets of its geology. He can visit the jewel-like mountain lakes— Solitude, Holly, and Amphitheater are just a few—cradled in high remote basins left by the Ice Age glaciers. He can get a closeup view of the Teton Glacier above Amphitheater Lake, or explore the Schoolroom Glacier, the tiny ice body below Hurricane Pass. He may follow the trail into Garnet Canyon to see the crystals from which the canyon takes its name and to examine the soaring ribbonlike black dike near the end of the trail. In Alaska Basin he can study the gently tilted layers of sandstone, limestone, and shale that once blanketed the entire Teton Range and can search for the fossils that help determine their age and decipher their history. From Hurricane Pass he can see how these even layers of sedimentary rock have been broken and displaced and how the older harder rocks that form the highest Teton peaks have been raised far above them along the Buck Mountain fault.

Of all those who explore the high country, it is the mountaineer who has perhaps the greatest opportunity to appreciate its geologic story. Indeed, the success of his climb and his very life may depend on an intuitive grasp of the mountain geology and the processes that shaped the peaks. He observes the most intimate details—the inclination of the joints and fractures, which gullies are swept by falling rocks, which projecting knobs are firm, and which cracks will safely take a piton. To many climbers the ascent of a peak is a challenge to technical competence, endurance, and courage, but to those endowed with curiosity and a sharp eye it can be much more. As he stands shoulder to shoulder with the clouds on some windswept peak, such as the Grand Teton, with the awesome panorama dropping away on all sides, he can hardly avoid asking how this came to be. What does the mountaineer see that inspires this curiosity? From the very first glance, it is apparent that the scenes to the north, south, east, and west are startlingly different.

Looking west from the rough, narrow, weather-ravaged granite summit of the Grand Teton, one sees far below him the layered gray cliffs of *marine sedimentary rocks* (solidified sediment originally deposited in a shallow arm of the ocean) overlapping the granite and dipping gently west, finally disappearing under the checkerboard farmland of Teton Basin. Still farther west are the rolling timbered slopes of the Big Hole Range in Idaho. A glance at the foreground, 3,000 feet below, shows some unusual relations of the streams to the mountains. The watershed divide of the Teton Range is not marked by the highest peaks as one would expect. Streams in Cascade Canyon and in other canyons to the north and south begin west of the peaks, bend around them, then flow eastward in deep narrow gorges cut through the highest part of the range, and emerge onto the flat floor of Jackson Hole.

In the view north along the crest of the Teton Range, the asymmetry of the mountains is most apparent. The steep east face culminating in the highest peaks contrasts with the lower more gentle west flank of the uplift. From the Grand Teton it is not possible to see the actual place where the mountains disappear under the lavas of Yellowstone Park, but the heavily timbered broad gentle surface of the lava plain is visible beyond the peaks and extends across the entire north panorama. Still farther north, 75 to 100 miles away, rise the snowcapped peaks (from northwest to northeast) of the Madison, Gallatin, and Beartooth Mountains.

The view east presents the greatest contrasts in the shortest distances—the flat floor of Jackson Hole is 3 miles away and 7,000 feet below the top of the Grand Teton. Along the junction of the mountains and valley floor are blue glacial lakes strung out like irregular beads in a necklace. They are conspicuously rimmed by black-appearing margins of pine trees that grow only on the surrounding glacial moraines. Beyond these are the broad treeless boulder-strewn plains of Jackson Hole. Fifty miles to the east and northeast, on the horizon beyond the rolling hills of the Pinyon Peak Highlands, are the horizontally layered volcanic rocks of the Absaroka Range. Southeast is the colorful red, purple, green, and gray Gros Ventre River Valley, with the fresh giant scar of the Lower Gros Ventre Slide near its mouth. Bounding the south side of this valley are the peaks of the Gros Ventre Mountains, whose tilted slabby gray cliff-forming layers resemble (and are the same as) those on the west flank of the Teton Range. Seventy miles away, in the southeast distance, beyond the Gros

Ventre Mountains are the shining snowcapped peaks of the Wind River Range, the highest peak of which (Gannett Peak) is about 20 feet higher than the Grand Teton.

Conspicuous on the eastern and southeastern skyline are high-level (11,000-12,000 feet) flat-topped surfaces on both the Wind River and Absaroka Ranges. These are remnants that mark the upper limit of sedimentary fill of the basins adjacent to the mountains. A plain once connected these surfaces and extended westward at least as far as the conspicuous flat on the mountain south of Lower Gros Ventre Slide. It is difficult to imagine the amount of rock that has been washed away from between these remnants in comparatively recent geologic time, during and after the rise of the Teton Range.

From this vantage point the mountaineer also gets a concept of the magnitude of the first and largest glaciers that scoured the landscape. Ice flowed southwestward in an essentially unbroken stream from the Beartooth Mountains, 100 miles away, westward from the Absaroka Range, and northwestward from the Wind River Range (fig. 57). Ice lapped up to treeline on the Teton Range and extended across Jackson Hole nearly to the top of the Lower Gros Ventre Slide. The Pinyon Peak and Mount Leidy Highlands were almost buried. All these glaciers came together in Jackson Hole and flowed south within the ever-narrowing Snake River Valley.

The view south presents a great variety of contrasts. Conspicuous, as in the view north, is the asymmetry of the range. South of the high peaks of crystalline rocks, gray layered cliffs of limestone extend in places all the way to the steep east face of the Teton Range where they are abruptly cut off by the great Teton fault.

The flat treeless floor of Jackson Hole narrows southward. Rising out of the middle are the previously described steepsided ice-scoured rocky buttes. Beginning near the town of Jackson, part of which is visible, and extending as far south as the eye can see are row upon row of sharp ridges and snowcapped peaks that converge at various angles. These are the Hoback, Wyoming, Salt River, and Snake River Ranges.

CARVING THE RUGGED PEAKS

The rugged grandeur of the Tetons is a product of four geologic factors: the tough hard rocks in the core, the amount of vertical uplift, the recency of the mountain-making movement, and the dynamic forces of destruction. Many other mountains in Wyoming have just as hard rocks in their cores and an equally great amount of vertical uplift, but they rose 50 to 60 million years ago and have been worn down by erosion from that time on. The Tetons, on the other hand, are the youngest range in Wyoming, less than 10 million years old, and have not had time to be so deeply eroded.

Steep mountain slopes—the perpetual battleground

Any steep slope or cliff is especially vulnerable to nature's methods of destruction. In the Tetons we see the never-ending struggle between two conflicting factors. The first is the extreme toughness of the rocks and their consequent resistance to erosion. The second is the presence of efficient transporting agencies that move out and away from the mountains all rock debris that might otherwise bury the lower slopes.

The rocks making up most of the Teton Range are among the hardest, toughest, and least porous known. Therefore, they resist mechanical disintegration by temperature changes, ice, and water. They consist predominantly of minerals that are subject to very little chemical decay in the cold climate of the Tetons.

Absence of weak layers prevents breaking of the tough rock masses under their own weight. All these conditions, then, are favorable for preservation of steep walls and high rock pinnacles. Nevertheless, they do break down. Great piles of broken rock *(talus)* that festoon the slopes of all the higher peaks bear witness to the unrelenting assault by the process of erosion upon the mountain citadels (figs. 4 and 31).

Rock disintegration and gravitational movement

A great variation in both daily and annual temperatures results in minute amounts of contraction and expan-

24

Figure 4. *Talus at the foot of the jagged frost-riven peaks around Ice Floe Lake in the south fork of Cascade Canyon. Photo by Philip Hyde.*

sion of rock particles. Repeated changes in volume produce stress and strain. Although the rocks in the Tetons are very dense, they eventually yield; a crack forms. Water which seeps in along this surface of weakness freezes, either overnight or during long cold spells, and expands, thereby prying a slab of rock away from the mountain wall. Repeated *frost wedging*, as the process is called, results eventually in tipping the slab so that it falls.

What happens to the rock slab? It may fall and roll several hundred or thousand feet, depending on the steepness of the mountain surface. Pieces are broken off as it encounters obstacles. All the fragments find their way to a valley floor or slope, where they momentarily come to rest.

Thus, rock debris is moved significant and easily observed distances by gravity.

None of this debris is stationary. If it is mixed with snow or saturated with water, the whole mass may slowly flow in the same manner as a glacier. These are called *rock glaciers*; some can be seen on the south side of Granite Canyon and one, nearly a mile long, is in the valley north of Eagles Rest Peak.

The countless snow avalanches that thunder down the mountain flanks after heavy winter snowfalls play their part, too, in gravitational transport. Loose rocks and debris are incorporated with the moving snow and borne down the mountainsides to the talus piles below. Trees, bushes, and soil are swept from the sites of the slides, leaving conspicuous scars down the slopes and exposing new rock surfaces to the attack of water and frost. Battered, broken, and uprooted trees along many of the canyon trails bear silent witness to the awesome power of snowslides.

These are some of the methods used by Nature in making debris and then, by means of gravity, clearing it from the mountain slopes. There are other ways, too. A weak layer of rock (usually one with a lot of clay in it), parallel to and underlying a mountain slope, may occur between two hard layers. An extended rainy spell may result in saturation of the weak zone so that it is well lubricated; then an earthquake or perhaps merely the weight of the overlying rock sends the now unstable mass cascading down the slope to the valley below. The famous Lower Gros Ventre Slide (fig. 5) was formed in this way on June 23, 1925.

Running water cuts and carries

Running water is another effective agent that transports rock debris and has helped dissect the Teton Range. The damage a broken water main can wreak on a roadbed is well known, as is the havoc of destructive floods. The spring floods of streams in the Tetons, swollen by melting snow and ice (annual precipitation, mostly snow, in the high parts would average a layer of water 5 feet thick), move some rock debris onto the adjoining floor of Jackson Hole.

Figure 5. *The Lower Gros Ventre slide, air oblique view south. The top of the scar is 2,000 feet above the river; the slide is more than a mile long and one-half mile wide. It dammed the Gros Ventre River in the foreground, impounding a lake about 200 feet deep and 5 miles long. Gros Ventre Mountains are in the distance. Photo by P. E. Millward.*

Now and then the range is deluged by summer cloudbursts. Water funnels down the maze of gullies on the mountainsides, quickly gathering volume and power, and plunges on to the talus slopes below, as if from gigantic hoses. The sudden onslaught of these torrents of water on the saturated unstable talus may trigger enormous rock and mudflows that carry vast quantities of material down into the canyons. During the summer of 1941 more than 100 of these flows occurred in the park.

Wherever water moves, it carries rock fragments varying in size from boulders to sand grains and on down to minute clay particles. *Erosion* (wearing away) by streams

27

is conspicuous wherever the water is muddy, as it always is each spring in the Snake, Buffalo Fork, and Gros Ventre Rivers. Clear mountain streams likewise can erode. Although the volume of material moved and the amount of downcutting of the stream bottom may not seem great in a single stream, the cumulative effect of many streams in an area, year after year and century after century, is enormous. Streams not only transport rocks brought to them by gravitational movement but also continually widen and deepen their valleys, thereby increasing the volume of transported debris.

The effectiveness of streams as transporting agents in the Tetons is enhanced by steep *gradients* (slopes); these increase water velocity which in turn expands the capability of the streams to carry larger and larger rock fragments.

Glaciers scour and transport

Mountain landscapes shaped by frost action, gravitational transport, and stream erosion alone generally have rounded summits, smooth slopes, and V-shaped valleys. The jagged ridges, sharply pointed peaks, and deep U-shaped valleys of the Tetons show that glaciers have played an important role in their sculpture. The small present-day glaciers still cradled in shaded recesses among the higher peaks (fig. 6) are but miniature replicas of great ice streams that occupied the region during the Ice Age. Evidence both here and in other parts of the world confirms that glaciers were once far more extensive than they are today.

Glaciers form wherever more snow accumulates during the winter than is melted during the summer. Gradually the piles of snow solidify to form ice, which begins to flow under its own weight. Rocks that have fallen from the surrounding ridges or have been picked up from the underlying bedrock are incorporated in the moving ice mass and carried along. The ability of ice to transport huge volumes of rock is easily observed even in the small present-day glaciers in the Tetons, all of which carry abundant rock fragments both on and within the ice.

Recent measurements show that the ice in the present

Figure 6. *The Teton Glacier on the north side of Grand Teton, air oblique view west. Photo by A. S. Post, August 19, 1963.*

Teton Glacier (fig. 6) moves nearly 30 feet per year. The ancient glaciers, which were much wider and deeper, may have moved as much as several hundred feet a year, like some of the large glaciers in Alaska.

As the glacier moves down a valley, it scours the valley bottom and walls. The efficiency of ice in this process is greatly increased by the presence of rock fragments which act as abrasives. The valley bottom is plowed, quarried, and swept clean of soil and loose rocks. Fragments of many sizes and shapes are dragged along the bottom of the moving ice and the hard ones scratch long parallel grooves in the underlying tough bedrock (fig. 7). Such grooves *(glacial striae)* record the direction of ice movement.

The effectiveness of glaciers in cutting a U-shaped valley is particularly striking in Glacier Gulch and Cascade Canyon (figs. 2 and 8).

The rock-walled amphitheater at the head of a glaciated valley is called a *cirque* (a good example is at the upper edge of the Teton Glacier, fig. 6). The steep cirque walls develop by frost action and by quarrying and abrasive action of the glacier ice where it is near its maximum thickness. Commonly the glacier scoops out a shallow basin in the floor of the cirque. Amphitheater Lake, Lake Solitude, Holly Lake, and many of the other small lakes high in the Teton Range are located in such basins.

The sharp peaks and the jagged knife-edge ridges so characteristic of the Tetons are divides left between cirques and valleys carved by the ancient glaciers.

Effects on Jackson Hole

Rock debris is carried toward the end of the glacier or along the margins where it is released as the ice melts. The semicircular ridge of rock fragments that marks the downhill margin of the glacier is called a *terminal moraine;* that along the sides is a *lateral moraine* (figs. 9 and 10). These are formed by the slow accumulation of material in the same manner as that at the end of a conveyor belt. They are not built by material pushed up ahead of the ice as if by a bulldozer. Large boulders carried by ice are called

30

Figure 7. *Rock surface polished and grooved by ice on the floor of Glacier Gulch.*

erratics; many of these are scattered on the floor of Jackson Hole and on the flanks of the surrounding mountains (fig. 11).

Great volumes of water pour from melting ice near the lower end of a glacier. These streams, heavily laden with rock flour produced by the grinding action of the glacier and with debris liberated from the melting ice, cut channels through the terminal moraine and spread a broad apron of gravel, sand, and silt down-valley from the glacier terminus (end). Material deposited by streams issuing from a glacier is called *outwash;* the sheet of outwash in front of the glacier is called an *outwash plain.* If the terminus is retreating, masses of old stagnant ice commonly are buried beneath the outwash; when these melt, the space they once occupied becames a deep circular or irregular depression called a *kettle* (fig. 12); many of these now contain small lakes or swamps.

As a glacier retreats, it may build a series of terminal moraines, marking pauses in the recession of the ice front. Streams issuing from the ice behind each new terminal moraine are incised more and more deeply into the older

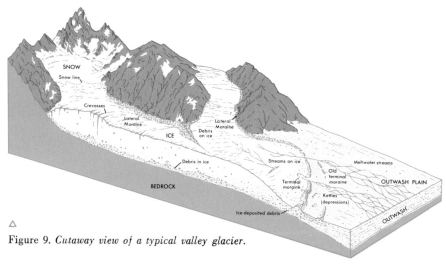

△

Figure 9. *Cutaway view of a typical valley glacier.*

Figure 8. *East face of the Teton Range showing some of the glacial features, air oblique view. Cascade Canyon, the U-shaped valley, was cut by ice. The glacier flowed toward the flats, occupied the area of Jenny Lake (foreground), and left an encircling ring of morainal debris, now covered with trees. The flat bare outwash plain in foreground was deposited by meltwater from the glacier. The lake occupies a depression that was left when the ice melted away. National Park Service photo by Bryan Harry.*

Figure 10. *Recently-built terminal moraine of the Schoolroom Glacier, a small ice mass near the head of the south fork of Cascade Canyon. The present glacier lies to the right just out of the field of view. The moraine marks a former position of the ice terminus; the lake (frozen over in this picture) occupies the depression left when the glacier wasted back from the moraine to its present position. Crest of the moraine stands about 50 feet above the lake level. Many of the lakes along the foot of the Teton Range occupy similar depressions behind older moraines. Photo by Philip Hyde.*

▽

Figure 11. *Large ice-transported boulder of coarse-grained pegmatite and granite resting on Cretaceous shale near Mosquito Creek, on the southwest margin of Jackson Hole. Many boulders at this locality are composed of pegmatite rock characteristic of the middle part of the Teton Range. This occurrence demonstrates that boulders 40 feet in diameter were carried southward 25 miles and left along the west edge of the ice stream, 1,500 feet above the base of the glacier on the floor of Jackson Hole.*

moraines and their outwash plains. Thus, new and younger layers of bouldery debris are spread at successively lower and lower levels. These surfaces are called *outwash terraces.*

Just as the jagged ridges, U-shaped valleys, and ice-polished rocks of the Teton Range attest the importance of glaciers in carving the mountain landscape, the flat gravel outwash plains and hummocky moraines on the floor of Jackson Hole demonstrate their efficiency in transporting debris from the mountains and shaping the scenery of the valley.

Glaciers sculptured all sides of Jackson Hole and filled it with ice to an elevation between 1,000 and 2,000

34

Figure 12. *"The Potholes," knob and kettle topography caused by melting of stagnant ice partly buried by outwash gravel. Air oblique view north from over Burned Ridge moraine (see fig. 61 for orientation). Photo by W. B. Hall and J. M. Hill.*

feet above the present valley floor. The visitor who looks eastward from the south entrance to the park can see clearly glacial scour lines that superficially resemble a series of terraces on the bare lower slopes of the Gros Ventre Mountains. Southward-moving ice cut these features in hard rocks. Elsewhere around the margins of Jackson Hole, especially where the rocks are soft, evidence that the landscape was shaped by ice has been partly or completely obliterated by later events. Rising 1,000 feet above the floor of Jackson Hole are several steepsided buttes (figs. 13 and 55) described previously, that represent "islands" of hard rock overridden and abraded by the ice. After the ice melted, these buttes were surrounded and partly buried by outwash debris.

The story of the glaciers and their place in the geologic history of the Teton region is discussed in more detail later in this booklet.

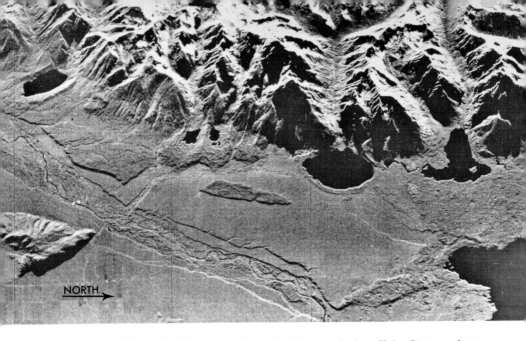

NORTH ➤

Figure 13. *Radar image of part of Tetons and Jackson Hole. Distance shown between left and right margins is 35 miles. Lakes from left to right: Phelps, Taggart, Bradley, Jenny, Leigh, Jackson. Blacktail Butte is at lower left. Channel of Snake River and outwash terraces are at lower left. Burned*

MOUNTAIN UPLIFT

Mountains appear ageless, but as with people, they pass through the stages of birth, youth, maturity, and old age, and eventually disappear. The Tetons are youthful and steep and are, therefore, extremely vulnerable to destructive processes that are constantly sculpturing the rugged features and carrying away the debris. The mountains are being destroyed. Although the processes of destruction may seem slow to us, we know they have been operating for millions of years—so why have the mountains not been leveled? How did they form in the first place?

Kinds of mountains

There are many kinds of mountains. Some are piles of lava and debris erupted from a volcano. Others are formed by the bowing up of the earth's crust in the shape of a giant dome or elongated arch. Still others are remnants of ac-

36

Ridge and Jackson Lake moraines are in center. Lava flows at upper right engulf north end of Tetons. Striated surfaces at lower right are glacial scour lines made by ice moving south from Yellowstone National Park. Image courtesy of National Aeronautics and Space Administration.

cumulated sedimentary rocks that once filled a basin between preexisting mountains and which are now partially worn away. An example of this type is the Absaroka Range 40 miles northeast of the Tetons (figs. 1 and 52).

The Tetons are a still different kind—a *fault block mountain range* carved from a segment of the earth's crust that has been uplifted along a fault. The *Teton fault* is approximately at the break in slope where the eastern foot of the range joins the flats at the west edge of Jackson Hole (see map inside back cover), but in most places is concealed beneath glacial deposits and debris shed from the adjacent steep slopes. The shape of the range and its relation to Jackson Hole have already been described. Clues as to the presence of the fault are: (1) the straight and deep east face of the Teton Range, (2) absence of foothills, (3) asymmetry of the range (fig. 14), and (4) small *fault scarps* (cliffs or steep slopes formed by faulting) along the mountain front (fig. 15).

37

Recent geophysical surveys of Jackson Hole combined with data from deep wells drilled in search of oil and gas east of the park also yield valuable clues. By measuring variations in the earth's magnetic field and in the pull of gravity and by studying the speed of shock waves generated by small dynamite explosions, Dr. John C. Behrendt of the U. S. Geological Survey has determined the depth and tilt of rock layers buried beneath the veneer of glacial debris and stream-laid sand and gravel on the valley floor. This information was used in constructing the geologic cross section in the back of the booklet. The same rock layers that cap the summit of Mount Moran (fig. 27) are buried at depths of nearly 24,000 feet beneath the nearby floor of Jackson Hole but are cut off by the Teton fault at the west edge of the valley. Thus the approximate amount of movement along the fault here would be about 30,000 feet.

Anatomy of faults

The preceding discussion shows that the Tetons are an upfaulted mountain block. Why is this significant? The extreme youth of the Teton fault, its large amount of displacement, and the fact that the newly upfaulted angular mountain block was subjected to intense glaciation are among the prime factors responsible for the development of the magnificent alpine scenery of the Teton Range. An un-

38

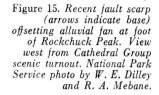

Figure 14. *Air oblique view south showing the width and asymmetry of Teton Range. Grand Teton is left of center and Mt. Moran is the broad humpy peak still farther left. Photo taken October 1, 1965.*

▷

Figure 15. *Recent fault scarp (arrows indicate base) offsetting alluvial fan at foot of Rockchuck Peak. View west from Cathedral Group scenic turnout. National Park Service photo by W. E. Dilley and R. A. Mebane.*

derstanding of the anatomy of faults is, therefore, pertinent.

A fault is a plane or zone in the earth's crust along which the rocks on one side have moved in relation to the rocks on the other. There are various kinds of faults just as there are various types of mountains. Three principal types of faults are present in the Teton region: normal faults, reverse faults, and thrust faults. A *normal fault* (fig. 16A) is a steeply *dipping* (steeply inclined) fault along which rocks above the fault have moved *down* relative to those beneath it. A *reverse fault* (fig. 16B) is a steeply inclined fault along which the rocks above the fault have moved *up* relative to those below it. A *thrust fault* (fig. 16C) is a gently inclined fault along which the principal movement has been more nearly horizontal than vertical.

Normal faults may be the result of tension or pulling apart of the earth's crust or they may be caused by adjustment of the rigid crust to the flow of semi-fluid material below. The crust sags or collapses in areas from which the subcrustal material has flowed and is bowed up and stretched in areas where excess subcrustal material has accumulated. In both areas the adjustments may result in normal faults.

Reverse faults are generally caused by compression of a rigid block of the crust, but some may also be due to lateral flow of subcrustal material.

39

Thrust faults are commonly associated with tightly bent or folded rocks. Many of them are apparently caused by severe compression of part of the crust, but some are thought to have formed at the base of slides of large rock masses that moved from high areas into adjacent low areas under the influence of gravity.

The Teton fault (see cross section inside back cover) is a normal fault; the Buck Mountain fault, which lies west of the main peaks of the Teton Range, is a reverse fault. No thrust faults have been recognized in the Teton Range, but the mountains south and southwest of the Tetons (fig. 1) display several enormous thrust faults along which masses of rocks many miles in extent have moved tens of miles eastward and northeastward.

Time and rate of uplift

When did the Tetons rise?

A study of the youngest sedimentary rocks on the floor of Jackson Hole shows that the Teton Range began to rise rapidly and take its present shape less than 9 million years ago. The towering peaks themselves are direct evidence that the rate of uplift far exceeded the rate at which the rising block was worn away by erosion. The mountains are still rising, and comparatively rapidly, as is indicated by small faults cutting the youngest deposits (fig. 15).

How rapidly? Can the rate be measured?

We know that in less than 9 million years (and probably in less than 7 million years) there has been 25,000 to 30,000 feet of displacement on the Teton fault. This is an average of about 1 foot in 300-400 years. The movement probably was not continuous but came as a series of jerks accompanied by violent earthquakes. One fault on the floor of Jackson Hole near the southern boundary of the park moved 150 feet in the last 15,000 years, an average of 1 foot per 100 years.

In view of this evidence of recent crustal unrest, it is not surprising that small earthquakes are frequent in the Teton region. More violent ones can probably be expected from time to time.

40

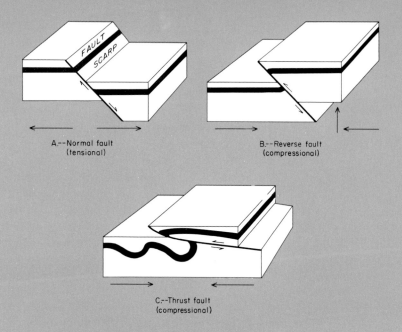

Figure 16. *Types of faults.*

Why are mountains here?

Why did the Tetons form where they are?

At the beginning of this booklet we discussed briefly the two most common theories of origin of mountains: continental drift and convection currents. The question of why mountains are where they are and more specifically why the Tetons are here remains a continuing scientific challenge regardless of the wealth of data already accumulated in our storehouse of knowledge.

The mobility of the earth's crust is an established fact. Despite its apparent rigidity, laboratory experiments demonstrate that rocks flow when subjected to extremely high pressures and temperatures. If the stress exceeds the strength at a given pressure and temperature, the rock breaks. Flowing and fracturing are two of the ways by which rocks adjust to the changing environments at various levels in the earth's crust. These acquired characteristics, some of which can be duplicated in the laboratory, are guides by which we interpret the geologic history of rocks that once were deep within the earth.

The site of the Teton block no doubt reflects hidden inequalities at depth. We cannot see these, nor in this area can we drill below the outer layer of the earth; nevertheless, measurements of gravity and of the earth's magnetic field clearly show that they exist.

We know that the Tetons rose at the time Jackson Hole collapsed but the volume of the uplifted block is considerably less than that of the downdropped block. This, then, was not just a simple case in which all the subcrustal material displaced by the sinking block was squeezed under the rising block (the way a hydraulic jack works). What happened to the rest of the material that once was under Jackson Hole? It could not be compressed so it had to go somewhere.

As you look northward from the top of the Grand Teton or Mount Moran, or from the main highway at the north edge of Grand Teton National Park, you see the great smooth sweep of the volcanic plateau in Yellowstone National Park. Farther off to the northeast are the strikingly layered volcanic rocks of the Absaroka Range (fig. 52). For these two areas, an estimate of the volume of volcanic rock that reached the surface and flowed out, or was blown out and spread far and wide by wind and water, is considerably in excess of 10,000 cubic miles. On the other hand, this volume is many times more than that displaced by the sagging and downfaulting of Jackson Hole.

Where did the rest of the volcanic material come from? Is it pertinent to our story? Teton Basin, on the west side of the Teton Range, and the broad Snake River downwarp farther to the northwest (fig. 1) are sufficiently large to have furnished the remainder of the volcanic debris. As it was blown out of vents in the Yellowstone-Absaroka area, its place could have been taken deep underground by material that moved laterally from below all three downdropped areas. The movement may have been caused by slow convection currents within the earth, or perhaps by some other, as yet unknown, force. The sagging of the earth's crust on both sides of the Teton Range as well as the long-continued volcanism are certainly directly related to the geologic history of the park.

42

In summary, we theorize as to how the Tetons rose and Jackson Hole sank but are not sure why the range is located at this particular place, why it trends north, why it rose so high, or why this one, of all the mountain ranges surrounding the Yellowstone-Absaroka volcanic area, had such a unique history of uplift. These are problems to challenge the minds of generations of earth scientists yet to come.

The restless land

Among the greatest of the park's many attractions is the solitude one can savor in the midst of magnificent scenery. Only a short walk separates us from the highway, torrents of cars, noise, and tension. Away from these, everything seems restful.

Quiescent it may seem, yet the landscape is not static but dynamic. This is one of the many exciting ideas that geology has contributed to society. The concept of the "everlasting hills" is a myth. All the features around us are actually rather short-lived in terms of geologic time. The discerning eye detects again and again the restlessness of the land. We have discussed many bits of evidence that show how the landscape and the earth's crust beneath it are constantly being carved, pushed up, dropped down, folded, tilted, and faulted.

The Teton landscape is a battleground, the scene of a continuing unresolved struggle between the forces that deform the earth's crust and raise the mountains and the slow processes of erosion that strive to level the uplands, fill the hollows, and reduce the landscape to an ultimate featureless plain. The remainder of this booklet is devoted to tracing the seesaw conflict between these inexorable antagonists through more than 2.5 billion years as they shaped the present landscape—and the battle still goes on.

Evidence of the struggle is all around us. Even though to some observers it may detract from the restfulness of the scene, perhaps it conveys to all of us a new appreciation of the tremendous dynamic forces responsible for the magnificence of the Teton Range.

The battle is indicated by the small faults that displace both the land surface and young deposits at the east base of

Mount Teewinot, Rockchuck Peak (fig. 15), and other places along the foot of the Tetons.

Jackson Hole continues to drop and tilt. The gravel-covered surfaces that originally sloped southward are now tilted westward toward the mountains. The Snake River, although the major stream, is not in the lowest part of Jackson Hole; Fish Creek, a lesser tributary near the town of Wilson, is 15 feet lower. For 10 miles this creek flows southward parallel to the Snake River but with a gentler gradient, thus permitting the two streams to join near the south end of Jackson Hole. As tilting continues, the Snake River west of Jackson tries to move westward but is prevented from doing so by long flood-control levees built south of the park.

Recent faults also break the valley floor between the Gros Ventre River and the town of Jackson.

The ever-changing piles of rock debris that mantle the slopes adjacent to the higher peaks, the creeping advance of rock glaciers, the devastating snow avalanches, and the thundering rockfalls are specific reminders that the land surface is restless. Jackson Hole contains more landslides and rock mudflows than almost any other part of the Rocky Mountain region. They constantly plague road builders (fig. 17) and add to the cost of other types of construction.

All of these examples of the relentless battle between constructive and destructive processes modifying the Teton landscape are but minor skirmishes. The bending and breaking of rocks at the surface are small reflections of enormous stresses and strains deep within the earth where the major conflict is being waged. It is revealed every now and then by a convulsion such as the 1959 earthquake in and west of Yellowstone Park. Events of this type release much more energy than all the nuclear devices thus far exploded by man.

Figure 17. *Slide blocking main highway in northern part of Grand Teton National Park. National Park Service photo by Eliot Davis, May 1952.*

ENORMOUS TIME AND DYNAMIC EARTH

Framework of time

One of geology's greatest philosophical contributions has been the demonstration of the enormity of geologic time. Astronomers deal with distances so great that they are almost beyond understanding; nuclear physicists study objects so small that we can hardly imagine them. Similarly, the geologist is concerned with spans of time so immense that they are scarcely comprehensible. Geology is a science of time as well as rocks, and in our geologic story of the Teton region we must refer frequently to the geologic time scale, the yardstick by which we measure the vast reaches of time in earth history.

Rocks and relative age

Very early in the science of geology it was recognized that in many places one can tell the comparative ages of rocks by their relations to one another. For example, most *sedimentary rocks* are consolidated accumulations of large or small rock fragments and were deposited as nearly hori-

45

zontal layers of gravel, sand, or mud. In an undisturbed sequence of sedimentary rocks, the layer on the bottom was deposited first and the layer on top was deposited last. All of these must, of course, be younger than any previously formed rock fragments incorporated in them.

Igneous rocks are those formed by solidification of molten material, either as lava flows on the earth's surface *(extrusive igneous rocks)* or at depth within the earth *(intrusive igneous rocks)*. The relative ages of extrusive igneous rocks can often be determined in much the same way as those of sedimentary strata. A lava flow is younger than the rocks on which it rests, but older than those that rest on top of it.

An intrusive igneous rock must be younger than the rocks that enclosed it at the time it solidified. It may contain pieces of the enclosing rocks that broke off the walls and fell into the liquid. Pebbles of the igneous rock that are incorporated in nearby sedimentary layers indicate that the sediments must be somewhat younger.

All of these criteria tell us only that one rock is older or younger than another. They tell us little about the absolute age of the rocks or about how much older one is than the other.

Fossils and geologic time

Fossils provide important clues to the ages of the rocks in which they are found. The slow evolution of living things through geologic time can be traced by a systematic study of fossils. The fossils are then used to determine the relative ages of the rocks that contain them and to establish a geologic time scale that can be applied to fossil-bearing rocks throughout the world. Figure 18 shows the major subdivisions of the last 600 million years of geologic time and some forms of life that dominated the scene during each of these intervals. Strata containing closely related fossils are grouped into *systems*; the time interval during which the strata comprising a particular system were deposited is termed a *period*. The periods are subdivisions of larger time units called *eras* and some are split into smaller time units called *epochs*. Strata deposited during an epoch comprise a *series*. Series are in turn subdivided into rock units called *groups* and formations. Expressed in tabular form these divisions are:

Subdivisions of geologic time	Time-rock units	Rock units
Era		
Period	System	
Epoch	Series	
		Group
		Formation

The time scale based on the study of fossil-bearing sedimentary rocks is called the stratigraphic time scale; it is given in table 1. The subdivisions are arranged in the same order in which they were deposited, with the oldest at the bottom and the youngest at the top. All rocks older than Cambrian (the first period in the Paleozoic Era) are classed as Precambrian. These rocks are so old that fossils are rare and therefore cannot be conveniently used as a basis for subdivision.

The stratigraphic time scale is extremely useful, but it has serious drawbacks. It can be applied only to fossil-bearing strata or to rocks whose ages are determined by their relation to those containing fossils. It cannot be used directly for rocks that lack fossils, such as igneous rocks, or metamorphic rocks in which fossils have been destroyed by heat or pressure. It is used to establish the relative ages of sedimentary strata throughout the world, but it gives no information as to how long ago a particular layer was deposited or how many years a given period or era lasted.

Radioactive clocks

The measurement of geologic time in terms of years was not possible until the discovery of natural radioactivity. It was found that certain atoms of a few elements spontaneously throw off particles from their nucleii and break down to form atoms of other elements. These decay processes take place at constant rates, unaffected by heat, pressure, or chemical conditions. If we know the rate at which a particular radioactive element decays, the length of time that has passed since a mineral crystal containing the elements formed can be calculated by comparing the amount of the radioactive element remaining in the crystal with the amount of disintegration products present.

47

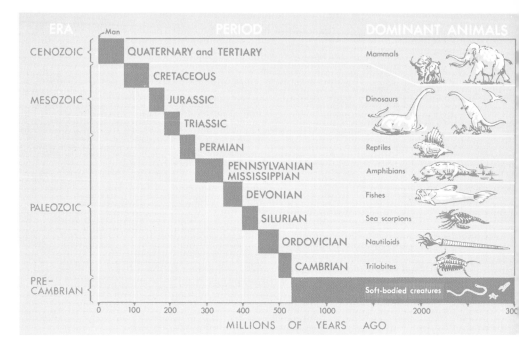

Figure 18. *Major subdivisions of the last 600 million years of geologic time and some of the dominant forms of life.*

Three principal radioactive clocks now in use are based on the decay of uranium to lead, rubidium to strontium, and potassium to argon. They are effective in dating minerals millions or billions of years old. Another clock, based on the decay of one type of carbon (*Carbon-14*) to nitrogen, dates organic material, but only if it is less than about 40,000 years old.

The uranium, rubidium, and potassium clocks are especially useful in dating igneous rocks. By determining the absolute ages of igneous rocks whose stratigraphic relations to fossil-bearing strata are known, it is possible to estimate the number of years represented by the various subdivisions of the stratigraphic time scale.

The yardstick of geologic time

Recent estimates suggest that the earth was formed at least 4.5 billion years ago. To visualize the length of geologic time and the relations between the stratigraphic and absolute time scales, let us imagine a yardstick as representing the length of time from the origin of the earth to the present (fig. 19). On one side of the yardstick we plot time

48

Era	System or period	Series or epoch
		Table 1. The stratigraphic time scale
Cenozoic	Quaternary	Recent
		Pleistocene
	Tertiary	Pliocene
		Miocene
		Oligocene
		Eocene
		Paleocene
Mesozoic	Cretaceous	
	Jurassic	
	Triassic	
Paleozoic	Permian	
	Pennsylvanian	
	Mississippian	
	Devonian	*The Silurian is the only major subdivision of the stratigraphic time scale not represented in Grand Teton National Park.*
	Silurian*	
	Ordovician	
	Cambrian	
	Precambrian	

in years; on the other, we plot the divisions of the stratigraphic time scale according to the most reliable absolute age determinations.

We are immediately struck by the fact that all of the subdivisions of the stratigraphic time scale since the beginning of the Paleozoic are compressed into the last 5 inches of our yardstick! All of the other 31 inches represent Precambrian time. We also see that subdivisions of the stratigraphic time scale do not represent equal numbers of years. We use smaller and smaller subdivisions as we approach the present. (Notice the subdivisions of the Tertiary and Quaternary in table 1 that are too small to show even in the enlarged part of figure 19). This is because the record of earth history is more vague and incomplete the farther back in time we go. In effect, we are very nearsighted in our view of time. This "geological myopia" becomes increasingly evident throughout the remainder of this booklet.

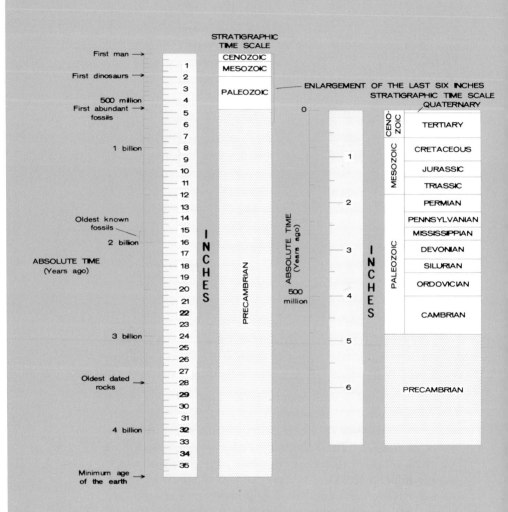

Figure 19. *The geologic time scale—our yardstick in time.*

PRECAMBRIAN ROCKS – THE CORE OF THE TETONS

The visitor who looks at the high, rugged peaks of the Teton Range is seeing rocks that record about seven-eighths of all geologic time. These Precambrian rocks are part of the very foundation of the continent and are therefore commonly referred to by geologists as basement rocks. In attempting to decipher their origin and history we peer backward through the dim mists of time, piecing together scattered clues to events that occurred billions of years ago, perhaps during the very birth of the North American Continent. To cite an oft-quoted example, it is as though we were attempting to read the history of an ancient and long-forgotten civilization from the scattered unnumbered pages of a torn manuscript, written in a language that we only partially understand.

Ancient gneisses and schists

The oldest Precambrian rocks in the Teton Range are layered gneisses and schists exposed over wide areas in the northern and southern parts of the range and as scattered isolated masses in the younger granite that forms the high peaks in the central parts. The layered gneisses may be seen easily along the trails in the lower parts of Indian Paintbrush and Death Canyons, and near Static Peak.

The *layered gneisses* are composed principally of quartz, feldspar, *biotite* (black mica), and *hornblende* (a very dark-green or black mineral commonly forming rodlike crystals). Distinct layers, a few inches to several feet thick, contain different proportions of these minerals and account for the banded appearance. Layers composed almost entirely of quartz and feldspar are light-gray or white, whereas darker gray layers contain higher proportions of biotite and hornblende.

Some layers are dark-green to black *amphibolite*, composed principally of hornblende but with a little feldspar and quartz. In many places the gneisses include layers of *schist*, a flaky rock, much of which is mica. At several places on the east slopes of Mount Moran thin layers

51

of impure gray marble are found interleaved with the gneisses. West of Static Peak along the Alaska Basin Trail a heavy dark rock with large amounts of *magnetite* (strongly magnetic black iron oxide) occurs as layers in the gneiss.

In some places the gneiss contains dark-reddish crystals of garnet as much as an inch in diameter. Commonly the garnet crystals are surrounded by white "halos" which lack biotite or hornblende, probably because the constituents necessary to form these minerals were absorbed by the garnet crystals. In Death Canyon and on the slopes of Static Peak some layers of gray gneiss contain egg-shaped masses of magnetite as much as one-half inch in diameter (fig. 20). These masses are likewise surrounded by elliptical white halos and have the startling appearance of small eyes peering from the rock. Appropriately, this rock has been called the "bright-eyed" gneiss by Prof. Charles C. Bradley in his published study (Wyoming Geological Association, 1956) of this area.

What were the ancient rocks from which the gneisses of the Teton Range were formed? Most of the evidence has been obliterated but a few remaining clues enable us to draw some general conclusions. The banded appearance of many of the gneisses suggests that they were formed from sedimentary and volcanic rocks that accumulated on the sea floor near a chain of volcanic islands—perhaps somewhat similar to the modern Aleutians or the islands of Indonesia. When these deposits were buried deep in the earth's crust the chemical composition of some layers may have undergone radical changes. Other layers, however, still have compositions resembling those of younger rocks elsewhere whose origins are better known. For example, the layers of impure marble were probably once beds of sandy limestone, and the lighter colored gneiss may have been muddy sandstone, possibly containing volcanic ash. Some dark amphibolite layers could represent altered lava flows or beds of volcanic ash; others may have resulted from the addition of silica to muddy magnesium-rich limestone during metamorphism. The magnetite-rich gneiss probably was originally a sedimentary iron ore.

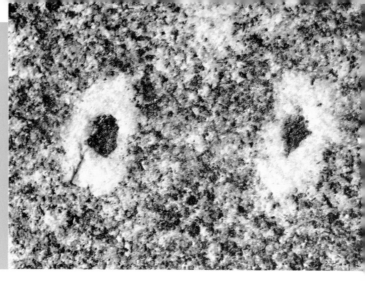

Figure 20. *"Bright-eyed" gneiss from Death Canyon. The dark magnetite spots are about ¼ inch in diameter. The surrounding gneiss is composed of quartz, feldspar, and biotite, but biotite is missing in the white halos around the magnetite.*

Minerals that were most easily altered at depth reacted with one another to form new minerals more "at home" under the high temperature and pressure in this environment just as the ingredients in a cake react when heated in an oven. Rocks formed by such processes are called *metamorphic rocks;* careful studies of the minerals that they contain suggest that the layered gneisses developed at temperatures as high as 1000°F at depths of 5 to 10 miles. Under these conditions the rocks must have behaved somewhat like soft taffy as is shown by layers that have been folded nearly double without being broken (fig. 21). Folds such as these range from fractions of an inch to thousands of feet across and are found in gneisses throughout the Teton Range. In a few places folds are superimposed in such a way as to indicate that the rocks were involved in several episodes of deformation in response to different sets of stress during metamorphism.

When did these gneisses form? Age determinations of minerals containing radioactive elements show that granite which was intruded into them after they were metamorphosed and folded is more than 2.5 billion years old. They must, therefore, be older than that. Thus, they probably are at least a billion years older than rocks containing the first faint traces of life on earth and 2 billion years older than the oldest rocks containing abundant fossils. How much older is not known, but the gneisses are certainly

Figure 21A. *Folds in layered gneisses. North face of the ridge west of Eagles Rest Peak. The face is about 700 feet high. Notice the extreme contortion of the gneiss layers.*

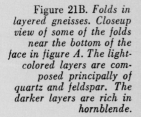

Figure 21B. *Folds in layered gneisses. Closeup view of some of the folds near the bottom of the face in figure A. The light-colored layers are composed principally of quartz and feldspar. The darker layers are rich in hornblende.*

among the oldest rocks in North America and record some of the earliest events in the building of this continent.

Irregular bodies of granite gneiss are interleaved with the layered gneisses in the northern part of the Teton Range. The *granite gneiss* is relatively coarse grained, streaky gray or pink, and composed principally of quartz, feldspar, biotite, and hornblende. It differs from enclosing layered gneisses in its coarser texture, lack of layering, and more uniform appearance. The dark minerals (biotite and

54

hornblende) are concentrated in thin discontinuous wisps that give the rock its streaky appearance.

The largest body of granite gneiss is exposed in a belt 1 to 2 miles wide and 10 miles long extending northeastward from near the head of Moran Canyon, across the upper part of Moose Basin, and into the lower reaches of Webb Canyon. This gneiss may have been formed from granite that invaded the ancient sedimentary and volcanic rocks before they were metamorphosed, or it may have been formed during metamorphism from some of the sediments and volcanics themselves.

At several places in Snowshoe, Waterfalls, and Colter Canyons the layered gneisses contain discontinuous masses a few tens or hundreds of feet in diameter of heavy darkgreen or black *serpentine*. This rock is frequently called *"soapstone"* because the surface feels smooth and soapy to the touch. Indians carved bowls (fig. 22) from similar material obtained from the west side of the Tetons and from the Gros Ventre Mountains to the southeast. Pebbles of serpentine along streams draining the west side of the Tetons have been cut and polished for jewelry and sold as *"Teton jade"*; it is much softer and less lustrous than real jade. The serpentine was formed by metamorphism of dark-colored igneous rocks lacking quartz and feldspar.

Granite and pegmatite

Contrary to popular belief, *granite* (crystalline igneous rock composed principally of quartz and feldspar) forms only a part of the Teton Range. The Grand Teton (fig. 6) and most surrounding subsidiary peaks are sculptured from an irregular mass of granite exposed continuously along the backbone of the range from Buck Mountain northward toward upper Leigh Canyon. The rock is commonly fine grained, white or light-gray, and is largely composed of crystals of gray quartz and white feldspar about the size and texture of the grains in very coarse lump sugar. Flakes of black or dark-brown mica (biotite) and silvery white mica *(muscovite)* about the size of grains of pepper are scattered through the rock.

From the floor of Jackson Hole the granite cliffs and

Figure 22. *Indian bowls carved from soapstone, probably from the Teton Range. Mouth of the unbroken bowl is about 4 inches in diameter.*

buttresses of the high peaks appear nearly white in contrast to the more somber grays and browns of surrounding gneisses and schists. These dark rocks are laced by a network of irregular light-colored granite dikes ranging in thickness from fractions of an inch to tens of feet (fig. 23).

The largest masses of granite contain abundant unoriented angular blocks and slabs of the older gneisses. These inclusions range from a few inches in diameter (fig. 24) to slabs hundreds of feet thick and thousands of feet long.

Dikes or irregular intrusions of pegmatite are found in almost every exposure of granite. *Pegmatite* contains the same minerals as granite but the individual mineral crystals are several inches or even as much as a foot in diameter.

Some pegmatites contain silvery plates or tabular crystals of muscovite mica as much as 6 inches across that can be split into transparent sheets with a pocket knife. Others have dark-brown biotite mica in crystals about the size and shape of the blade of a table knife.

A few pegmatites contain scattered red-brown crystals of garnet ranging in size from that of a BB shot to a small marble; a few in Garnet Canyon and Glacier Gulch are larger than baseballs (fig. 25). The garnets are fractured and many are partly altered to *chlorite* (a dull-green micaceous mineral) so they are of no value as gems.

Pegmatite *dikes* (tabular bodies of rock that, while still molten, were forced along fractures in older rocks)

Figure 23A. *Dikes of granite and pegmatite. Network of light-colored granite dikes on the northeast face of the West Horn on Mt. Moran. The dikes cut through gneiss in which the layers slant steeply downward to the left. The face is about 700 feet high. Snowfield in the foreground is at the edge of the Falling Ice Glacier.*

Figure 23B. *Dikes of granite and pegmatite. Irregular dike of granite and pegmatite cutting through dark layered gneisses near Wilderness Falls in Waterfalls Canyon. The cliff face is about 80 feet high. Contacts of the dike are sharp and angular and cut across the layers in the enclosing gneiss.* ▷

Figure 24. *Angular blocks of old streaky granite gneiss in fine-grained granite northwest of Lake Solitude. The difference in orientation of the streaks in the gneiss blocks indicates that the blocks have been rotated with respect to one another and that the fine-grained granite must therefore have been liquid at the time of intrusion. A small light-colored dike in the upper left-hand block of gneiss ends at the edge of the block; it intruded the gneiss before the block was broken off and incorporated in the granite. A small dike of pegmatite cuts diagonally through the granite just to the left of the hammer and extends into the blocks of gneiss at both ends. This dike was intruded after the granite had solidified. Thus, in this one small exposure we can recognize four ages of rocks: the streaky granite gneiss, the light-colored dike, the fine-grained granite, and the small pegmatite dike.*

commonly cut across granite dikes, but in many places the reverse is true. Some dikes are composed of layers of pegmatite alternating with layers of granite (fig. 26), showing that the pegmatite and granite are nearly contemporaneous. Prof. Bruno Giletti and his coworkers at Brown University, using the rubidium-strontium radioactive clock, determined that the granite and pegmatite in the Teton Range are about 2.5 billion years old.

Black dikes

Even the most casual visitor to the Teton Range notices the remarkable black band that extends down the east face

58

Figure 25. *Garnet crystal in pegmatite. The crystal is about 6 inches in diameter. Other minerals are feldspar (white) and clusters of white mica flakes. The mica crystals appear dark in the photograph because they are wet.*

of Mount Moran (figs. 27 and 28) from the summit and disappears into the trees north of Leigh Lake. This is the outcropping edge of a steeply inclined dike composed of *diabase*, a nearly black igneous rock very similar to basalt. Thinner diabase dikes are visible on the east face of Middle Teton, on the south side of the Grand Teton, and in several other places in the range (see geologic map inside back cover).

The diabase is a heavy dark-greenish-gray to black rock that turns rust brown on faces that have been exposed to the weather. It is studded with small lath-shaped crystals of feldspar that are greenish gray in the fresh rock and milk white on weathered surfaces.

The black dikes formed from molten rock that welled up into nearly vertical fissures in the older Precambrian

Figure 26. *A small dike of pegmatite and granite cutting through folded layered gneiss in Death Canyon. Coarse-grained pegmatite forms most of the dike, but fine-grained granite is found near the center. Small offshoots of the dike penetrate into the wall rocks. The dike cuts straight across folds in the enclosing gneisses and must therefore have been intruded after development of the folds. The white ruler is about 6 inches long.*

rocks. Toward the edges of the dikes the feldspar laths in the diabase become smaller and smaller (fig. 29), indicating that the wall rocks were relatively cool when the *magma* or melted rock was intruded. Rapid chilling at the edges prevented growth of large crystals. In many places hot solutions from the dike permeated the wall rocks, staining them rosy red.

The black dike on Mount Moran is about 150 feet thick near the summit of the peak. This dike has been traced westward for more than 7 miles. Where it passes out of the park south of Green Lakes Mountain it is 100 feet thick. The amount of molten material needed to form the exposed segment of this single dike could fill Jenny Lake three times over. The other dikes are thinner and not as long: the dike on Middle Teton is 20 to 40 feet thick, and the dike on Grand Teton is 40 to 60 feet thick.

Figure 27. Air oblique view of the east face of Mt. Moran, showing the great black dike. Main mass of the mountain is layered gneiss and streaky granite gneiss. White lines are dikes of granite and pegmatite; light-gray mound on the summit is about 50 feet of Cambrian sedimentary rock (Flathead Sandstone). Notice that the black dike cuts across the dikes of granite and pegmatite but that its upper edge is covered by the much younger layer of sandstone. Falling Ice Glacier is in the left center; Skillet Glacier is in the lower right center. Photo by A. S. Post. University of Washington, August 19, 1963.

Figure 28. *The great black dike on the east face of Mt. Moran. The dike is about 150 feet thick and its vertical extent in the picture is about 3,000 feet. The fractures in the dike perpendicular to its walls are cracks formed as the liquified rock cooled and crystallized. Falling Ice Glacier is in the center. National Park Service photo by H. D. Pownall.*

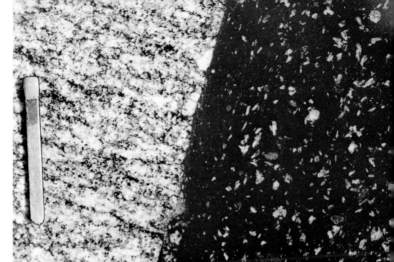

Figure 29. *Closeup view of the edge of the Middle Teton black dike exposed on the north wall of Garnet Canyon near the west end of the trail. Dike rock (diabase) is on the right; wall rock (gneiss) is on the left. Match shows scale.*

The black dikes must be the youngest of the Precambrian units because they cut across all other Precambrian rocks. The dikes must have been intruded before the beginning of Cambrian deposition inasmuch as they do not cut the oldest Cambrian beds. Gneiss adjacent to the dike on Mount Moran contains biotite that was heated and altered about 1.3 billion years ago according to Professor Giletti. The alteration is believed to have occurred when the dike was emplaced; therefore this and similar dikes elsewhere in the range are probably about 1.3 billion years old.

Quartzite

At about the same time as the dikes were being intruded in the Tetons, many thousands of feet of sedimentary rocks, chiefly sandstone, were deposited in western Montana, 200 miles northwest of Grand Teton National Park. The sandstone was later recrystallized and recemented and became a very dense hard rock called *quartzite*. Similar quartzite, possibly part of the same deposit, was laid down west of the north end of the Teton Range, within the area now called the Snake River downwarp (fig. 1).

The visitor who hikes or camps anywhere on the floor of Jackson Hole becomes painfully aware of the thousands upon thousands of remarkably rounded hard quartzite boulders. He wonders where they came from because nowhere in the adjacent mountains is this rock type exposed. The answer is that the quartzites were derived from a long-

63

vanished uplift (figs. 42 and 46), carried eastward by powerful rivers past the north end of the Teton Range, and then were deposited in a vast sheet of gravel that covered much of Jackson Hole 60 to 80 million years ago. Since then, these virtually indestructible boulders have been re-worked many times by streams and ice, yet still retain the characteristics of the original ancient sediments.

A backward glance

So far we have seen that the Precambrian basement exposed in the Teton Range contains a complex array of rocks of diverse origins and various ages. Before passing on to the younger rocks, reference to our yardstick may help to place the Precambrian events in their proper perspective.

In all of Precambrian time, which encompasses more than 85 percent of the history of the earth (31 of the 36 inches of our yardstick), only two events are dated in the Teton Range: the intrusion of granite and pegmatite about 2.5 billion years ago, and the emplacement of the black dikes about 1.3 billion years ago. These dates are indicated by heavy arrows on the time scale (fig. 30). The ancient gneisses and schists were formed sometime before 2.5 billion years ago, and probably are no older than 3.5 billion years, the age of the oldest rocks dated anywhere in the world.

The close of the Precambrian—end of the beginning

More than 700 million years elapsed between intrusion of the black dikes and deposition of the first Paleozoic sedimentary rocks — a longer period of time than has elapsed since the beginning of the Paleozoic Era. During this enormous interval the Precambrian rocks were uplift-ed, exposed to erosion, and gradually worn to a nearly featureless plain, perhaps somewhat resembling the vast flat areas in which similar Precambrian rocks are now ex-posed in central and eastern Canada. At the close of Pre-cambrian time, about 600 million years ago, the plain slow-ly floundered and the site of the future Teton Range disap-peared beneath shallow seas that were to wash across it in-

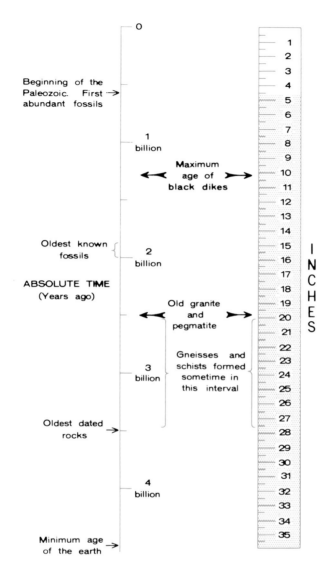

Figure 30. *A glance at the yardstick.*
The geologic time scale shows positions
of principal events recorded in the
Precambrian rocks of the Tetons.

termittently for the next 500 million years. It is to the
sediments deposited in these seas that we turn to read the
next chapter in the geologic story of the Teton Range.

65

The Paleozoic sequence

North, west, and south of the highest Teton peaks the soaring spires and knife-edge ridges of Precambrian rock give way to rounded spurs and lower flat-topped summits, whose slopes are palisaded by continuous gray cliffs that resemble the battlements of some ancient and long-abandoned fortress (fig. 31). As mentioned previously, the cliffs are the projecting edges of layers of sedimentary rocks of Paleozoic age that accumulated in or along the margins of shallow seas. At one time the layers formed a thick unbroken, nearly horizontal blanket across the Precambrian basement rocks, but subsequent uplift of the eastern edge of the Teton fault block tilted them westward. They were then stripped from the highest peaks.

The Paleozoic and younger sedimentary rocks in the Teton region are subdivided into *formations*, each of which is named. A formation is composed of rock layers which, because of their similar physical characteristics, can be distinguished from overlying and underlying layers. They must be thick enough to be shown on a geologic map. Table 2 lists the various Paleozoic formations present in and adjacent to Grand Teton National Park and gives their thicknesses and characteristics. These sedimentary rocks are of special interest, for they not only record an important chapter of geologic history but elsewhere in the region they contain petroleum and other mineral deposits.

The Paleozoic rocks can be viewed close at hand from the top of the Teton Village tram (fig. 32) on the south boundary of the park. A less accessible but equally spectacular exposure of Paleozoic rocks is in Alaska Basin, along the west margin of the park, where they are stacked like even layers in a gigantic cake (fig. 33).

Alaska Basin—site of an outstanding rock and fossil record

Strata in Alaska Basin record with unusual clarity the opening chapters in the chronicle of seas that flowed and

66

Figure 31. *Paleozoic rocks on the west flank of the Teton Range, air oblique view west. Ragged peaks in the foreground (Buck Mountain on the left center, Mt. Wister, with top outlined by snow patch on the extreme right), are carved in Precambrian rocks. Banded cliffs in the background are sedimentary rocks. Alaska Basin is at upper right. Teton Basin, a broad, extensively farmed valley in eastern Idaho, is at top. Photo by A. S. Post, University of Washington, 1963.*

ebbed across the future site of the Teton Range during most of the Paleozoic Era. In the various rock layers are inscribed stories of the slow advance and retreat of ancient shorelines, of the storm waves breaking on long-vanished beaches, and of the slow and intricate evolution of the myriads of sea creatures that inhabited these restless waters.

Careful study of the fossils allows us to determine the age of each formation (table 3). Even more revealing, the fossils themselves are tangible evidence of the orderly parade of life that crossed the Teton landscape during more than 250 million years. Here is a record of Nature's experiments with life, the triumphs, failures, the bizarre, the beautiful.

67

Table 2. — Paleozoic sedimentary rocks exposed in the Teton region.

Age	Formation	Thickness (feet)	Description	Where exposed
Permian	Phosphoria Formation	150-250	Dolomite, gray, cherty, sandy, black shale and phosphate beds; marine.	North and west flanks of Teton Range, north flank of Gros Ventre Mountains, southern Jackson Hole
Pennsylvanian	Tensleep and Amsden Formations	600-1,500	Tensleep Sandstone, light-gray, hard, underlain by Amsden Formation, a domolite and red shale with a basal red sandstone; marine.	North and west flanks of Teton Range, north flank of Gros Ventre Mountains, southern Jackson Hole
Mississippian	Madison Limestone	1,000-1,200	Limestone, blue-gray, hard, fossiliferous; thin red shale in places near top; marine.	North and west flanks of Teton Range, north flank of Gros Ventre Mountains, southern Jackson Hole
Devonian	Darby Formation	200-500	Dolomite, dark-gray to brown, fetid, hard, and brown, black, and yellow shale; marine	North and west flanks of Teton Range, north flank of Gros Ventre Mountains, southern Jackson Hole
Ordovician	Bighorn Dolomite	300-500	Dolomite, light-gray, siliceous, very hard; white dense very fine-grained dolomite at top; marine.	North and west flanks of Teton Range, north and west flanks of Gros Ventre Mountains, southern Jackson Hole
Cambrian	Gallatin Limestone	180-300	Limestone, blue-gray, hard, thin-bedded; marine.	North and west flanks of Teton Range and Gros Ventre Mountains.
	Gros Ventre Formation	600-800	Shale, green, flaky, with Death Canyon Limestone Member composed of about 300 feet of hard cliff-forming limestone in middle; marine.	North and west flanks of Teton Range and Gros Ventre Mountains.
	Flathead Sandstone	175-200	Sandstone, reddish-brown, very hard, brittle; partly marine.	North and west flanks of Teton Range and Gros Ventre Mountains.

The regularity and parallel relations of the layers in well-exposed sections such as the one in Alaska Basin suggest that all these rocks were deposited in a single uninterrupted sequence. However, the fossils and regional distribution of the rock units show that this is not really the case. The incomplete nature of this record becomes apparent if we plot the ages of the various formations on the absolute geologic time scale (fig. 34). The length of time from the beginning of the Cambrian Period to the end of the Mississippian Period is about 285 million years. The strata in Alaska Basin are a record of approximately 120 million years. More than half of the pages in the geologic story are missing even though, compared with most other areas, the book as a whole is remarkably complete! During these unrecorded intervals of time either no sediments were

Figure 32. *Paleozoic marine sedimentary rocks near south boundary of Grand Teton National Park. View is south from top of Teton Village tram. National Park Service photo by W. E. Dilley and R. A. Mebane.*

deposited in the area of the Teton Range or, if deposited, they were removed by erosion.

Advance and retreat of Cambrian seas: an example

The first invasion and retreat of the Paleozoic sea are sketched on figure 35. Early in Cambrian time a shallow seaway, called the *Cordilleran trough*, extended from southern California northeastward across Nevada into Utah and Idaho (fig. 35A). The vast gently rolling plain on Precambrian rocks to the east was drained by sluggish westward-flowing rivers that carried sand and mud into the sea. Slow subsidence of the land caused the sea to spread gradually eastward. Sand accumulated along the beaches just as it does today. As the sea moved still farther east, mud was deposited on the now-submerged beach sand. In the Teton area, the oldest sand deposit is called the Flathead Sandstone (fig. 36).

The mud laid down on top of the Flathead Sandstone as the shoreline advanced eastward across the Teton area is now called the Wolsey Shale Member of the Gros Ventre

69

Figure 33. *View southwest across Alaska Basin, showing tilted layers of Paleozoic sedimentary rocks on the west flank of the Teton Range. National Park Service photo.*

Formation. Some shale shows patterns of cracks that formed when the accumulating mud was briefly exposed to the air along tidal flats. Small phosphatic-shelled animals called *brachiopods* inhabited these lonely tidal flats (fig. 37A and B) but as far as is known, nothing lived on land. Many shale beds are marked with faint trails and borings of wormlike creatures, and a few contain the remains of tiny very intricately developed creatures with head, eyes, segmented body, and tail. These are known as *trilobites* (fig. 37C and D). Descendants of these lived in various seas that crossed the site of the dormant Teton Range for the next 250 million years.

As the shoreline moved eastward, the Death Canyon Limestone Member of the Gros Ventre Formation (fig. 33) was deposited in clear water farther from shore. Following this the sea retreated to the west for a short time. In the shallow muddy water resulting from this retreat the Park Shale Member of the Gros Ventre Formation was deposited. In places underwater "meadows" of algae flourished on the sea bottom and built extensive reefs (fig. 38A). From time

AGE (Numbers show age in millions of years)		FORMATION (Thickness)	ROCKS AND FOSSILS
(310) MISSISSIPPIAN		MADISON LIMESTONE (Total about 1,100 feet, but only lower 300 feet preserved in this section)	Uniform thin beds of blue-gray limestone and sparse very thin layers of shale. Brachiopods, corals, and other fossils abundant.
(345) LATE AND MIDDLE DEVONIAN (390)		DARBY FORMATION (About 350 feet)	Thin beds of gray and buff dolomite interbedded with layers of gray, yellow, and black shale. A few fossil brachiopods, corals, and bryozoans.
(425) LATE AND MIDDLE ORDOVICIAN (440)		BIGHORN DOLOMITE (About 450 feet; Leigh Dolomite Member about 40 feet thick at top)	Thick to very thin beds of blue-gray or brown dolomite, white on weathered surfaces. A few broken fossil brachiopods, bryozoans, and horn corals. Thin beds of white fine-grained dolomite at top are the Leigh Member.
(500) LATE CAMBRIAN (530)		GALLATIN LIMESTONE (180 feet)	Blue-gray limestone mottled with irregular rusty or yellow patches. Trilobites and brachiopods.
MIDDLE CAMBRIAN	GROS VENTRE FORMATION	PARK SHALE MEMBER (220 feet)	Gray-green shale containing beds of platy limestone conglomerate. Trilobites, brachiopods, and fossil algal heads.
		DEATH CANYON LIMESTONE MEMBER (285 feet)	Two thick beds of dark-blue-gray limestone separated by 15 to 20 feet of shale that locally contains abundant fossil brachiopods and trilobites.
		WOLSEY SHALE MEMBER (100 feet)	Soft greenish-gray shale containing beds of purple and green sandstone near base. A few fossil brachiopods.
(570)		FLATHEAD SANDSTONE (175 feet)	Brown, maroon, and white sandstone, locally containing many rounded pebbles of quartz and feldspar. Some beds of green shale at top.
PRECAMBRIAN			Granite, gneiss, and pegmatite.

Table 3. *Formations exposed in Alaska Basin.*

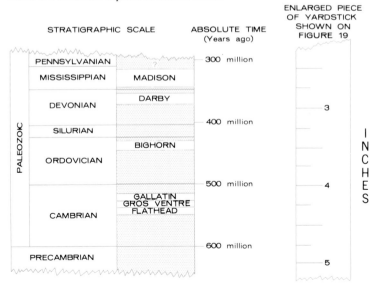

Figure 34. *Absolute ages of the formations in Alaska Basin. Shaded parts of the scale show intervals for which there is no record.*

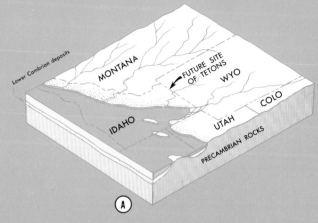

Figure 35A. *The first invasions of the Paleozoic sea. In Early Cambrian time an arm of the Pacific Ocean occupied a deep trough in Idaho, Nevada, and part of Utah. The land to the east was a broad gently rolling plain of Precambrian rocks drained by sluggish westward-flowing streams. The site of the Teton Range was part of this plain. Slow subsidence of the land caused the sea to move eastward during Middle Cambrian time flooding the Precambrian plain.*

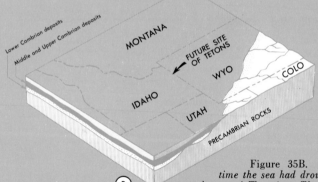

Figure 35B. *By Late Cambrian time the sea had drowned all of Montana and most of Wyoming. The Flathead Sandstone and Gros Ventre Formation were deposited as the sea advanced. The Gallatin Limestone was being deposited when the shoreline was in about the position shown in this drawing.*

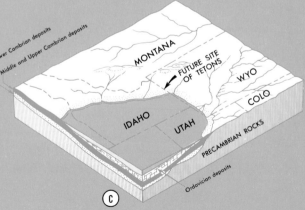

Figure 35C. *In Early Ordovician time uplift of the land caused the sea to retreat back into the trough, exposing the Cambrian deposits to erosion. Cambrian deposits were partly stripped off of some areas. The Bighorn Dolomite was deposited during the next advance of the sea in Middle and Late Ordovician time.*

Figure 36. *Conglomeratic basal bed of Flathead Sandstone and underlying Precambrian granite gneiss: contact is indicated by a dark horizontal line about 1 foot below hammer. This contact is all that is left to mark a 2-billion year gap in the rock record of earth history. The locality is on the crest of the Teton Range 1 mile northwest of Lake Solitude.*

to time shoal areas were hit by violent storm waves that tore loose platy fragments of recently solidified limestone and swept them into nearby channels where they were buried and cemented into thin beds of jumbled fragments (fig. 38B) called *"edgewise" conglomerate.* These are widespread in the shale and in overlying and underlying limestones.

Once again the shoreline crept eastward, the seas cleared, and the Gallatin Limestone was deposited. The Gallatin, like the Death Canyon Limestone Member, was laid down for the most part in quiet, clear water, probably at depths of 100 to 200 feet. However, a few beds of "edgewise" conglomerate indicate the occurrence of sporadic storms. At this time, the sea covered all of Idaho and Montana and most of Wyoming (fig. 35B) and extended eastward across the Dakotas to connect with shallow seas that covered the eastern United States. Soon after this maximum stage was reached slow uplift caused the sea to retreat gradually westward. The site of the Teton Range emerged above the waves, where, as far as is now known, it may have been exposed to erosion for nearly 70 million years (fig. 35C).

The above historical summary of geologic events in Cambrian time is recorded in the Cambrian formations. This is an example of the reconstructions, based on the sedimentary rock record, that have been made of the Paleozoic systems in this area.

Younger Paleozoic formations

Formations of the remaining Paleozoic systems are likewise of interest because of the ways in which they differ

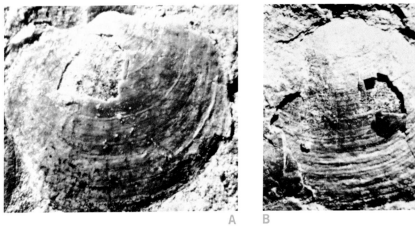

A   B

Figure 37. *Cambrian fossils in Grand Teton National Park.*
A-B. *Phosphatic-shelled brachiopods, the oldest fossils found in the park. Actual width of specimens is about ¼ inch.*
C-D. *Trilobites. Width of C is ¼ inch, D is ½ inch. National Park Service photos by W. E. Dilley and R. A. Mebane.*

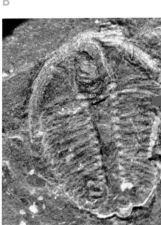

C

D

Figure 38A. *Distinctive features of Cambrian rocks. Algal heads in the Park Shale Member of the Gros Ventre Formation. These calcareous mounds were built by algae growing in a shallow sea in Cambrian time. They are now exposed on the divide between North and South Leigh Creeks, nearly 2 miles above sea level!*

▷

Figure 38B. *Distinctive features of Cambrian rocks. Bed of "edgewise" conglomerate in the Gallatin Limestone. Angular plates of solidified lime-ooze were torn from the sea bottom by storm waves, swept into depressions, and then buried in lime mud. These fragments, seen in cross section, make the strange design on the rock. Thin limestone beds below are undisturbed. National Park Service photo by W. E. Dilley.*

from those already described.

The Bighorn Dolomite of Ordovician age forms ragged hard massive light-gray to white cliffs 100 to 200 feet high (figs. 32 and 33). *Dolomite* is a calcium-magnesium carbonate, but the original sediment probably was a calcium carbonate mud that was altered by magnesium-rich sea water shortly after deposition. Corals and other marine animals were abundant in the clear warm seas at this time.

Dolomite in the Darby Formation of Devonian age differs greatly from the Bighorn Dolomite; that in the Darby is dark-brown to almost black, has an oily smell, and contains layers of black, pink, and yellow mudstone and thin sandstone. The sea bottom during deposition of these rocks was foul and frequently the water was turbid. Abundant fossil fragments indicate fishes were common for the first time. Exposures of the Darby Formation are recognizable by their distinctive dull-yellow thin-layered slopes between the prominent gray massive cliffs of formations below and above.

The Madison Limestone of Mississippian age is 1,000 feet thick and is exposed in spectacular vertical cliffs along canyons in the north, west, and south parts of the Tetons. It is noted for the abundant remains of beautifully preserved marine organisms (fig. 39). The fossils and the relatively pure blue-gray limestone in which they are embedded indicate deposition in warm tranquil seas. The beautiful Ice Cave on the west side of the Tetons and all other major caves in the region were dissolved out of this rock by underground water.

The Pennsylvanian System is represented by the Amsden Formation and the Tensleep Sandstone. Cliffs of the Tensleep Sandstone can be seen along the Gros Ventre River at the east edge of the park. The Amsden, below the Tensleep, consists of red and green shale, sandstone, and thin limestone. The shale is especially weak and slippery when exposed to weathering and saturated with water. These are the strata that make up the glide plane of the Lower Gros Ventre Slide (fig. 5) east of the park.

The Phosphoria Formation and its equivalents of Permian age are unlike any other Paleozoic rocks because of their extraordinary content of uncommon elements. The formation consists of sandy dolomite, widespread black phosphate beds and black shale that is unusually rich not only in phosphorus, but also in vanadium, uranium, chromium, zinc, selenium, molybdenum, cobalt, and silver. The formation is mined extensively in nearby parts of Idaho and in Wyoming for phosphatic fertilizer, for the chemical element phosphorus, and for some of the metals that can be derived from the rocks as byproducts. These elements and compounds are not everywhere concentrated enough to be of economic interest, but their dollar value is, in a regional sense, comparable to that of some of the world's greatest mineral deposits.

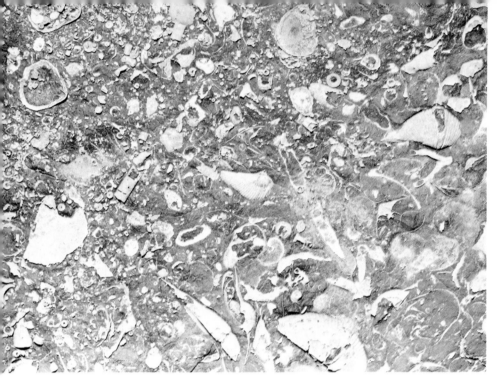

Figure 39. *A glimpse of the sea floor during deposition of the Madison Limestone 330 million years ago, showing the remains of brachiopods, corals, and other forms of life that inhabited the shallow warm water.*

A. *Slab in which fossils are somewhat broken and scattered. Scale slightly reduced. National Park Service photo by W. E. Dilley and R. A. Mebane.*

B. *Slab in which fossils are remarkably complete. Silver dollar gives scale. Specimen is in University of Wyoming Geological Museum.*

The Mesozoic Era in the Teton region was a time of alternating marine, transitional, and continental environments. Moreover, the highly diversified forms of life, ranging from marine mollusks to tremendous, land-living dinosaurs, confirm and reinforce the story of the rocks. Living things, too, were in transition, for as environment changed, many forms moved from the sea to land in order to survive. It was the time when some of the most spectacularly colored rock strata of the region were deposited.

Colorful first Mesozoic strata

Bright-red soft Triassic rocks more than 1,000 feet thick, known as the Chugwater Formation, comprise most of the basal part of the Mesozoic sequence (table 4). They form colorful hills east and south of the park. The red color is caused by a minor amount of iron oxide. Mud cracks and the presence of fossil reptiles and amphibians indicate deposition in a tidal flat environment, with the sea lying several miles southwest of Jackson Hole. A few beds of white *gypsum* (calcium sulfate) are present; they were apparently deposited during evaporation of shallow bodies of salt water cut off from the open sea.

As the Triassic Period gave way to the Jurassic, salmon-red windblown sand (Nugget Sandstone) spread across the older red beds and in turn was buried by thin red shale and thick gypsum deposits of the Gypsum Spring Formation. Then down from Alaska and spreading across most of Wyoming came the *Sundance Sea*, a warm, muddy, shallow body of water that teemed with marine mollusks. In it more than 500 feet of highly fossiliferous soft gray shale and thin limestones and sandstones were deposited. The sea withdrew and the Morrison and Cloverly Formations (Jurassic and Lower Cretaceous) were deposited on low-lying tropical humid flood plains. These rocks are colorful, consisting of red, pink, purple, and green badland-forming claystones and mudstones, and yellow to buff sandstones. Vegetation was abundant and large and small dinosaurs roamed the countryside or inhabited the swamps.

Table 4. — Mesozoic sedimentary rocks exposed in the Teton region.				
Age	Formation	Thickness (feet)	Description	Where exposed
CRETACEOUS	Harebell Formation	0-5,000	Sandstone, olive drab, silty, drab siltstone, and dark-gray shale; thick beds of quartzite pebble conglomerate in upper part.	Eastern and northeastern parts of Jackson Hole.
	Meeteetse Formation	0-700	Sandstone, gray to chalky white, blue-green to gray siltstone, thin coal, and green to yellow bentonite.	Spread Creek area.
	Mesaverde Formation	0-1,000	Sandstone, white, massive, soft, thin gray shale, sparse coal.	Eastern Jackson Hole.
	Unnamed sequence of lenticular sandstone, shale, and coal.	3,500±	Sandstone and shale, gray to brown; abundant coal in lower 2,000 feet.	Eastern Jackson Hole and eastern margin of the park.
	Bacon Ridge Sandstone	900-1,200	Sandstone, light gray, massive, marine, gray shale, many coal beds.	Eastern Jackson Hole and eastern margin of the park.
	Cody Shale	1,300-2,200	Shale, gray, soft; thin green sandstone, some bentonite; marine.	Eastern and northern parts of Jackson Hole.
	Frontier Formation	1,000	Sandstone, gray, and black to gray shale, marine; many persistent white bentonite beds in lower part.	Eastern and northern parts and southwestern margin of Jackson Hole.
	Mowry Shale	700	Shale, silvery-gray, hard, siliceous, with many fish scales; thin bentonite beds; marine.	Gros Ventre River Valley, northern margin of the park, and southern part of Jackson Hole.
	Thermopolis Shale	150-200	Shale, black, soft, fissile, with persistent sandstone at top; marine.	Gros Ventre River Valley, northern margin of the park, and southern part of Jackson Hole
JURASSIC	Cloverly and Morrison(?) Formations	650	Sandstone, light gray, sparkly, rusty near top, underlain by variegated soft claystone; basal part is silty dully-variegated sandstone and claystone.	North end of Teton Range and Gros Ventre River Valley.
	Sundance Formation	500-700	Sandstone, green, underlain by soft gray shale and thin highly fossiliferous limestones; marine.	North end of Teton Range, Blacktail Butte, Gros Ventre River Valley.
	Gypsum Spring Formation	75-100	Gypsum, white, interbedded with red shale and gray dolomite; partly marine.	North end of Teton Range, Blacktail Butte, Gros Ventre River Valley.
TRIASSIC	Nugget Sandstone	0-350	Sandstone, salmon-red, hard.	North flank of Gros Ventre Mountains, southern Jackson Hole.
	Chugwater Formation	1,000-1,500	Siltstone and shale, red, thin-bedded; one thin marine limestone in upper third.	North flank of Gros Ventre Mountains, north end of Teton Range, southernmost Jackson Hole.
	Dinwoody Formation	200-400	Siltstone, brown, hard, thin-bedded, marine.	North flank of Gros Ventre Mountains, north end of Teton Range, southernmost Jackson Hole.

The youngest division of the Mesozoic Era is the Cretaceous Period. Near the beginning of this period, brightly colored rocks continued to be deposited. Then, the Teton region, as well as most of Wyoming, was partly, and at times completely, submerged by shallow muddy seas. As a result, the brightly variegated strata were covered by 10,000 feet of generally drab-colored sand, silt, and clay containing some coal beds, volcanic ash layers, and minor amounts of gravel.

The Cretaceous sea finally retreated eastward from the Teton region about 85 million years ago, following the deposition of the Bacon Ridge Sandstone (fig. 40). As it withdrew, extensive coal swamps developed along the sea coast. The record of these swamps is preserved in coal beds 5 to 10 feet thick in the Upper Cretaceous deposits. The coal beds are now visible in abandoned mines along the east margin of the park. Coal is formed from compacted plant debris; about 5 feet of this material is needed to form 1 inch of coal. Thus, lush vegetation must have flourished for long periods of time, probably in a hot wet climate similar to that now prevailing in the Florida Everglades.

Sporadically throughout Cretaceous time fine-grained ash was blown out of volcanoes to the west and northwest and deposited in quiet shallow water. Subsequently the ash was altered to a type of clay called *bentonite* that is used in the foundry industry and in oil well drilling muds. In Jackson Hole, the elk and deer lick bentonite exposures to get a bitter salt and, where the beds are water-saturated, enjoy "stomping" on them. Bentonite swells when wet and causes many landslides along access roads into Jackson Hole (fig. 17).

The Cretaceous rocks in the Teton region are part of an enormous east-thinning wedge that here is nearly 2 miles thick. Most of the debris was derived from slowly rising mountains to the west.

Cretaceous sedimentary rocks are much more than of just scientific interest; they contain mineral deposits important to the economy of Wyoming and of the nation.

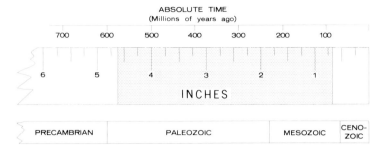

Figure 40. *The yardstick and the sea. The shaded part of the yardstick shows the 500-million-year interval during which Paleozoic and Mesozoic seas swept intermittently across the future site of the Tetons. When they finally withdrew about 85 million years ago, a little more than ⅝ of an inch of the yardstick remained to be accounted for.*

Wyoming leads the States in production of bentonite, all of it from Cretaceous rocks. These strata have yielded far more oil and gas than any other geologic system in the State and the production is geographically widespread. They also contain enormous coal reserves, some in beds between 50 and 100 feet thick. The energy resources alone of the Cretaceous System in Wyoming make it invaluable to our industrialized society.

As the end of the Cretaceous Period approached, slightly more than 80 million years ago, the flat monotonous landscape (fig. 41) which had prevailed during most of Late Cretaceous time gave little hint that the stage was set for one of the most exciting and important chapters in the geologic history of North America.

Birth of the Rocky Mountains

The episode of mountain building that resulted in formation of the ancestral Rocky Mountains has long been known as the *Laramide Revolution*. West and southwest of Wyoming, mountains had already formed, the older ones as far away as Nevada and as far back in time as Jurassic, the younger ones rising progressively farther east, like

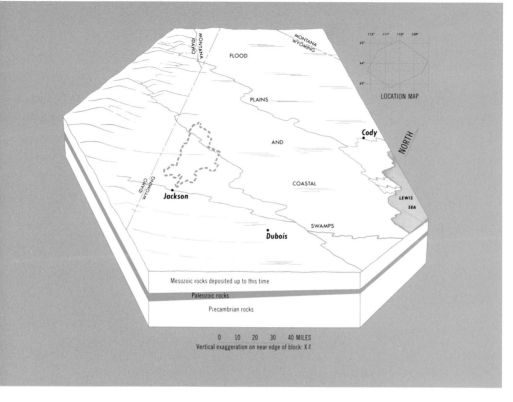

Figure 41. *Grand Teton National Park region slightly more than 80 million years ago, just before onset of Laramide Revolution. The last Cretaceous sea still lingered in central Wyoming.*

giant waves moving toward a coast. The first crustal movement in the Teton area began in latest Cretaceous time when a broad low northwest-trending arch developed in the approximate area of the present Teton Range and Gros Ventre Mountains. However, this uplift bore no resemblance to the Tetons as we know them today for the present range formed 70 million years later.

One bit of evidence (there are others) of the first Laramide mountain building west of the Tetons is a tremendous deposit of quartzite boulder debris (several hundred cubic miles in volume) derived from the *Targhee uplift* (fig. 42). Nowhere is the uplift now exposed, but from the size, composition, and distribution of rock fragments that came from it, we know that it was north and west of the northern end of the present-day Teton Range. Powerful streams carried boulders, sand, and clay eastward and

83

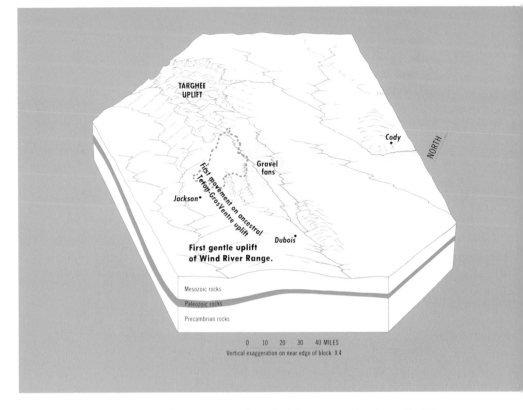

Figure 42. *Teton region at the end of Cretaceous time about 65 million years ago. The ancestral Teton-Gros Ventre uplift had risen and prominent southeastward drainage from the Targhee uplift was well established. See figure 41 for State lines and location map.*

southeastward across the future site of Jackson Hole and deposited them in the Harebell Formation (table 4). Mingled with this sediment were tiny flakes of gold and a small amount of mercury. Fine-grained debris was carried still farther east and southeast into two enormous depositional troughs in central and southern Wyoming. Most of the large rock fragments were derived from Precambrian and possibly lower Paleozoic quartzites. This means that at least 15,000 feet of overlying Paleozoic and Mesozoic strata must first have been stripped away from the Targhee uplift before the quartzites were exposed to erosion.

Remains of four-legged horned ceratopsian dinosaurs,

84

Figure 43. *Triceratops, a horned dinosaur of the type that inhabited Jackson Hole about 65 million years ago. Sketch by S. H. Knight.*

possibly *Triceratops* (fig. 43), reflecting the last population explosion of these reptiles, have been found in pebbly sandstone of the Harebell Formation in highway cuts on the Togwotee Pass road 8 miles east of the park.

Near the end of Cretaceous time, broad gentle uplifts also began to stir at the sites of future mountain ranges in many parts of Wyoming. The ancestral Teton-Gros Ventre arch continued to grow. Associated with and parallel to it was a series of sharp steepsided elongated northwest-trending upfolds *(anticlines)*. One of these can be seen where it crosses the highway at the Lava Creek Campground near the eastern margin of Grand Teton National Park.

During these episodes of mountain building, erosion, and deposition, the dinosaurs became extinct all over the world. The "Age of Mammals" was about to begin.

TERTIARY—TIME OF MAMMALS, MOUNTAINS, LAKES, AND VOLCANOES

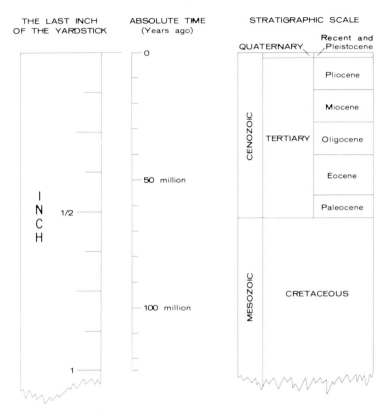

Figure 44. *The last inch of the yardstick, enlarged to show subdivisions of the Cenozoic Era.*

The Cenozoic (table 1), last and shortest of the geologic eras, comprises the Tertiary and Quaternary Periods. It began about 65 million years ago and is represented by only the final one-half inch of our imaginary yardstick of time (fig. 19). Nevertheless, it is the era during which the Tetons rose in their present form and the landscape was sculptured into the panorama of beauty that we now see. In order to show the many Tertiary and Quaternary events in the Teton region, it is necessary to enlarge greatly the last part of the yardstick (fig. 44). There are two reasons for

Table 5. — Cenozoic sedimentary rocks and unconsolidated deposits exposed in the Teton region.

Age	Formation	Thickness (feet)	Description	Where exposed
Recent	Modern stream, land-slide, glacial and talus deposits	0-200±	Sand, gravel, and silt along present streams; jumbled broken rock in landslides and on talus slopes; debris around existing glaciers.	Floor of Jackson Hole and in canyons and on mountain-sides throughout the region.
Pleistocene	Glacial deposits and loess	0-200±	Gravel, sand, silt, and glacial debris.	Floor of Jackson Hole.
Pleistocene	Unnamed upper lake sequence	0-500	Shale, brown-gray, sandstone, and conglomerate.	Gros Ventre River Valley.
Pleistocene	Unnamed lower lake sequence	0-200	Shale, siltstone, and sandstone, gray, green, and red.	National Elk Refuge.
Pleistocene or Pliocene	Bivouac Formation	0-1,000	Conglomerate, with purplish-gray welded tuff in upper part.	Signal Mountain and West Gros Ventre Butte.
Pliocene	Teewinot Formation	0-6,000	Limestone, tuff, and claystone, white, soft.	National Elk Refuge, Black-tail Butte, and eastern margin of Antelope Flat.
Pliocene	Camp Davis Formation	0-5,500	Conglomerate, red and gray, with white tuff, diatomite, and red and white claystone.	Southernmost tip of Jackson Hole.
Miocene	Colter Formation	0-7,000	Volcanic conglomerate, tuff, and sand-stone, white to green-brown, with locally-derived basalt and andesite rock fragments.	Pilgrim and Ditch Creeks, and north end of Teton Range.
Oligocene	Wiggins Formation	0-3,000	Volcanic conglomerate, gray to brown, with white tuff layers.	Eastern margin of Jackson Hole.
Eocene	Unnamed upper and middle Eocene sequence	0-1,000	Tuff, conglomerate, sandstone, and claystone, green, underlain by variegated claystone and quartzite pebble conglomerate.	Eastern margin of Jackson Hole.
Eocene	Wind River and Indian Meadows Formations	2,000-3,000	Claystone and sandstone, variegated, and locally-derived conglomerate; persistent coal and gray shale zone in middle.	Eastern margin of Jackson Hole.
Paleocene	Unnamed greenish-gray and brown sandstone and claystone sequence	1,000-2,000	Sandstone and claystone, greenish-gray and brown, intertonguing at base with quartzite pebble conglomerate.	Eastern margin of Jackson Hole.
Paleocene	Pinyon Conglomerate	500-5,000	Conglomerate, brown, chiefly of rounded quartzite; coal and clay-stone locally at base.	Eastern part of Jackson Hole, Mt. Leidy and Pinyon Peak Highlands, and north end of Teton Range.

the extraordinarily clear and complete record. First, the Teton region was a relatively active part of the earth's crust, characterized by many downdropped blocks. The number of events is great and their records are preserved in sediments trapped in the subsiding basins. Second, the geologically recent past is much easier to see than the far dimmer, distant past; the rocks that record later events are fresher, less altered, more complete, and more easily interpreted than are those that tell us of older events.

87

Figure 45. *Pinyon Conglomerate of Paleocene age, along the northwest margin of the Teton Range.*

During the early part of the Tertiary Period, mountain building and basin subsidence were the dominant types of crustal movement. Seas retreated southward down the Mississippi Valley and never again invaded the Teton area. Environments on the recently uplifted land were diverse and favorable for the development of new forms of plants and animals.

Rise and burial of mountains

The enormous section of Tertiary sedimentary rocks in the Jackson Hole area (table 5) is one of the most impressive in North America. If the maximum thicknesses of all formations were added, they would total more than 6 miles, but nowhere did this amount of rock accumulate in a single unbroken sequence. No other region in the United States contains a thicker or more complete nonmarine Tertiary record; many areas have little or none. The accumulation in Jackson Hole reflects active uplifts of nearby mountains that supplied abundant rock debris, concurrent

88

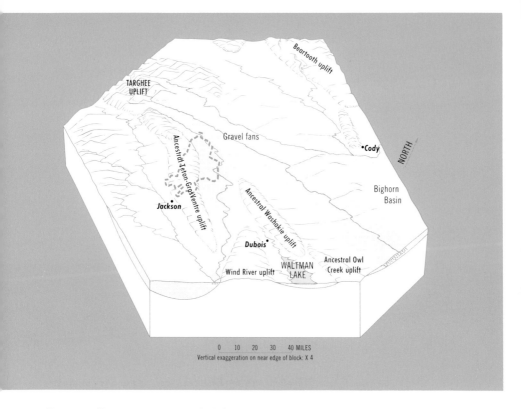

Figure 46. *Teton region near end of deposition of Paleocene rocks, slightly less than 60 million years ago. The ancestral Teton-Gros Ventre uplift formed a partial barrier between the Jackson Hole and Green River depositional basins; major drainages from the Targhee uplift spread an enormous sheet of gravel for 100 miles to the east. See figure 41 for State lines and location map.*

sinking of nearby basins in which the sediments could be preserved, and proximity to the great Yellowstone-Absaroka volcanic area, one of the most active continental volcanic fields in the United States. The volume and composition of the Tertiary strata are, therefore, clear evidence of crustal and subcrustal instability.

The many thick layers of conglomerate are evidence of rapid erosion of nearby highlands. The Pinyon Conglomerate (fig. 45), for example, contains zones as much as 2,500 feet thick of remarkably well-rounded pebbles, cobbles, and boulders, chiefly of quartzite identical with that in the underlying Harebell Formation and derived from the same source, the Targhee uplift. Like the Harebell the matrix contains small amounts of gold and mer-

89

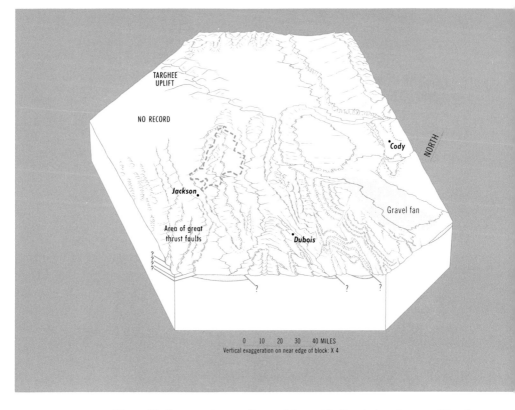

Figure 47. *Teton region at climax of Laramide Revolution, between 50 and 55 million years ago. See figure 41 for State lines and location map.*

cury. Rock fragments increase in size northwestward toward the source area (fig. 46) and most show percussion scars, evidence of ferocious pounding that occurred during transport by powerful, swift rivers and steep gradients.

Conglomerates such as the Pinyon are not the only clue to the time of mountain building. Another type of evidence—faults—is demonstrated in figure 16. The youngest rocks cut by a fault are always older than the fault. Many faults and the rocks on each side are covered by still younger unbroken sediments. These must, therefore, have been deposited after fault movement ceased. By dating both the faulted and the overlying unbroken sediments, the time of fault movement can be bracketed.

Observations of this type in western Wyoming indicate that the Laramide Revolution reached a climax during

90

earliest Eocene time, 50 to 55 million years ago. Mountain-producing upwarps formed during this episode were commonly bounded on one side by either reverse or thrust faults (fig. 16B and C) and intervening blocks were downfolded into large, very deep basins. The amount of movement of the mountain blocks over the basins ranged from tens of miles in the Snake River, Salt River, Wyoming, and Hoback Ranges directly south of the Tetons to less than 5 miles on the east margin of Jackson Hole (the west flank of the Washakie Range shown in figure 1). The ancestral Teton-Gros Ventre uplift continued to rise but remained one of the less conspicuous mountain ranges in the region (fig. 47).

The Buck Mountain fault, the great reverse fault which lies just west of the highest Teton peaks (see geologic map and cross section), was formed either at this time or during a later episode of movement that also involved the southwest margin of the Gros Ventre Mountains. The Buck Mountain fault is of special importance because it raised a segment of Precambrian rocks several thousand feet. Later, when the entire range as we now know it was uplifted by movement along the Teton fault, the hard basement rocks in this previously upfaulted segment continued to stand much higher than those in adjacent parts of the range. All of the major peaks in the Tetons are carved from this doubly uplifted block.

The brightly colored sandstone, mudstone, and claystone in the Indian Meadows and Wind River Formations (lower Eocene) in the eastern part of Jackson Hole were derived from variegated Triassic, Jurassic, and Lower Cretaceous rocks exposed on the adjacent mountain flanks. Fossils in these Eocene Formations show that it took less than 10 million years for the uplifts to be deeply eroded and partially buried in their own debris.

The Laramide Revolution in the area of Grand Teton National Park ended during Eocene time between 45 and 50 million years ago, and as the mountains and basins became stabilized a new element was added. Volcanoes broke through to the surface in many parts of the Yellowstone-

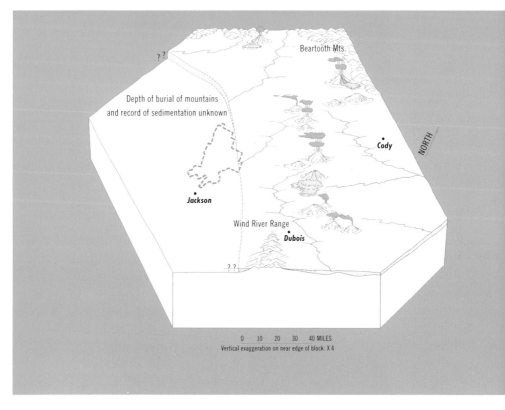

Figure 48. *Teton region near the close of Oligocene deposition, between 25 and 30 million years ago, showing areas of major volcanoes and lava flows. See figure 41 for State lines and location map.*

Absaroka area and the constantly increasing volume of their eruptive debris was a major factor in the speed of filling of basins and burial of mountains throughout Wyoming. This entire process only took about 20 million years, and along the east margin of Jackson Hole it was largely completed during Oligocene time (fig. 48). However, east and northeast of Jackson Lake a Miocene downwarp subsequently formed and in it accumulated at least 7,000 feet of locally derived sediments of volcanic origin.

Teewinot Lake (fig. 49), the first big freshwater lake in Jackson Hole, was formed during Pliocene time, about 10 million years ago, and in it the Teewinot Formation was deposited. These lake strata consist of more than 5,000 feet of white limestone, thin-bedded claystone, and *tuff*

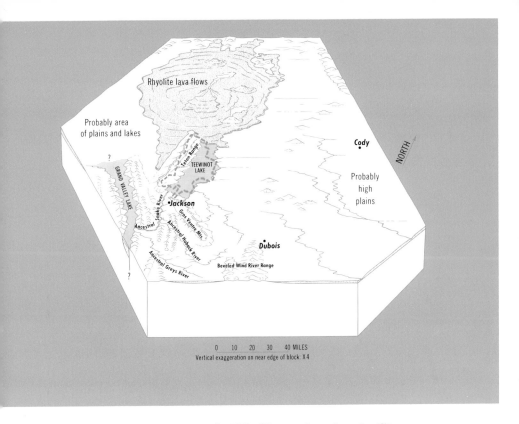

Figure 49. *Teton region near close of middle Pliocene time, about 5 million years ago, showing areas of major volcanoes and lava flows. See figure 41 for State lines and location map.*

(solidified ash made up of tiny fragments of volcanic rock and splinters of volcanic glass). The claystones contain fossil snails, clams, beaver bones and teeth, aquatic mice, suckers, and other fossils that indicate deposition in a shallow freshwater lake environment. These beds underlie Jackson Lake Lodge, the National Elk Refuge, part of Blacktail Butte, and are conspicuously exposed in white outcrops that look like snowbanks on the upper slopes along the east margin of the park across the valley from the Grand Teton.

Teewinot Lake was formed on a down-faulted block and was dammed behind (north of) a fault that trends east across the floor of Jackson Hole at the south boundary of the park. Lakes are among the most short-lived of earth features because the forces of nature soon conspire to fill

93

Figure 50. *Restoration of a middle Eocene landscape showing some of the more abundant types of mammals. Mural painting by Jay H. Matterness; photo courtesy of the Smithsonian Institution.*

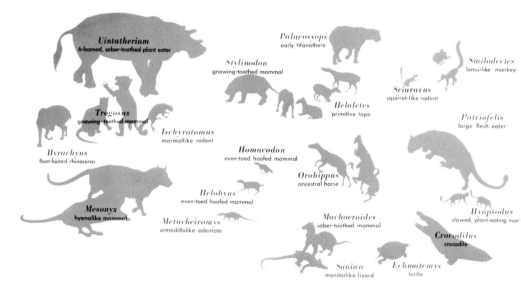

Uintatherium
6-horned, saber-toothed plant eater

Palaeosyops
early titanothere

Stylinodon
gnawing-toothed mammal

Smilodectes
lemurlike monkey

Sciuravus
squirrel-like rodent

Helaletes
primitive tapir

Trogosus
gnawing-toothed mammal

Patriofelis
large flesh eater

Ischyrotomus
marmotlike rodent

Hyrachyus
fleet-footed rhinoceros

Homacodon
even-toed hoofed mammal

Orohippus
ancestral horse

Mesonyx
hyenalike mammal

Helohyus
even-toed hoofed mammal

Hyopsodus
clawed, plant-eating mammal

Metacheiromys
armadillolike edentate

Machaeroides
saber-toothed mammal

Crocodilus
crocodile

Saniwa
monitorlike lizard

Echmatemys
turtle

them up or empty them. This lake existed for perhaps 5 million years during middle Pliocene time; it was shallow, and remained so despite the pouring in of a mile-thick layer of sediment. This indicates that downdropping of the lake floor just about kept pace with deposition.

Other lakes formed in response to similar crustal movements in nearby places. One such lake, *Grand Valley Lake* (fig. 49), formed about 25 miles southwest of Teewinot Lake; both contained sediments with nearly the same thickness, composition, appearance, age, and fossils. Although these two lakes are on opposite sides of the Snake River Range, the ancestral Snake River apparently flowed through a canyon previously cut across the range and provided a direct connection between them.

Development of mammals

The Cenozoic Era is known as the "Age of Mammals." Small mammals had already existed, though quite inconspicuously, in Wyoming for about 90 million years before Paleocene time. Then about 65 million years ago their proliferation began as a result of the extinction of dinosaurs, obliteration of seaways that were barriers to distribution, and the development of new and varied types of environment. These new environments included savannah plains, low hills and high mountains, freshwater lakes and swamps, and extensive river systems. The mammals increased in size and, for the first time, became abundant in numbers of both species and individuals. The development and widespread distribution of grasses and other forage on which many of the animals depended were highly significant. Successful adaption of *herbivores* (vegetation-eating animals) led, in turn, to increased varieties and numbers of predatory *carnivores* (meat-eating animals).

During early Eocene time, coal swamps formed in eastern Jackson Hole and persisted for thousands of years, as is shown by 60 feet of coal in a single bed at one locality. Continuing on into middle Eocene time, the climate was subtropical and humid, and the terrain was near sea level. Tropical breadfruits, figs, and magnolias flourished along with a more temperate flora of redwood, hickory, maple,

95

Figure 51. *A typical Oligocene landscape showing some of the more abundant types of mammals. Mural painting by Jay H. Matterness; photo courtesy of Smithsonian Institution.*

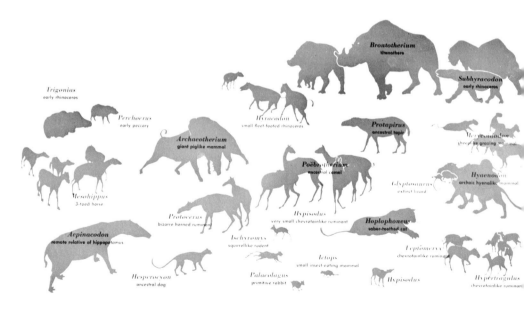

and oak. Horses the size of a dog and many other small mammals were abundant. Primates, thriving in an ideal forest habitat, were numerous. Streams contained gar fish and crocodiles (fig. 50).

Early in the Oligocene Epoch, between 30 and 35 million years ago, the climate in Jackson Hole became cooler and drier, and the subtropical plants gave way to the warm temperate flora of oak, beech, maple, alder, and ash. The general land surface rose higher above sea level, perhaps by accumulation of several thousand feet of Oligocene volcanic rocks (fig. 52) rather than by continental uplift. *Titanotheres* (large four-legged mammals with the general size and shape of a rhinoceros) flourished in great numbers for a few million years and then abruptly vanished. Horses by now were about the size of a very small modern colt. Rabbits, rodents, carnivores, tiny camels, and other mammals were abundant in Jackson Hole, and the fauna, surprisingly, was essentially the same as that 500 miles to the east, at a much lower elevation, on the plains of Nebraska and South Dakota (fig. 51).

The Miocene Epoch (15 to 25 million years ago) was the time of such intense volcanic activity in the Teton region that animals must have found survival very difficult. A few skeletons and fragmentary parts of camels about the size of a small horse and other piglike animals called *oreodonts* comprise our only record of mammals; nothing is known of the plants. Farther east the climate fluctuated from subtropical to warm temperate, gradually becoming cooler toward the end of the epoch.

Fossils in the Pliocene lake deposits (8 to 10 million years old; see description of Teewinot Formation) include shallow-water types of snails, clams, diatoms, and ostracodes, as well as beavers, mice, suckers, and frogs. Pollen in these beds show that adjacent upland areas supported fir, spruce, pine, juniper, sage, and other trees and shrubs common to the area today. Therefore, the climate must have been much cooler than in Miocene time. No large mammals of Pliocene age have been found in Jackson Hole. The record of life during Quaternary time is discussed later.

Figure 52. *Layers of volcanic conglomerate separated by thin white tuff beds in Wiggins Formation. These cliffs, on the north side of Togwotee Pass, are about 1,100 feet high and represent a cross section of part of the enormous blanket of waterlaid debris that spread south and east from the Yellowstone-Absaroka volcanic area. These and younger deposits from the same general source filled the basins and almost completely buried the mountains in this part of Wyoming.*

Volcanoes

Volcanoes are one of the most interesting parts of the geologic story of the Teton region. Although ash from distant volcanoes had settled in northwestern Wyoming at least as far back in time as Jurassic, the first nearby active volcanoes (since the Precambrian) erupted in the Yellowstone-Absaroka region during the early Eocene, about 50 million years ago. From then on, the volcanic area grew in size and the violence of eruptions and volume of debris increased until Pliocene time. This debris had a profound influence on the color and composition of the sediments and on the environment and types of plants and animals.

The color of the volcanic rocks and the sediments derived from them varies significantly from one epoch to

98

Figure 53. *Air oblique view south, showing the north end of the Teton Range disappearing beneath Pleistocene lava flows. Light-colored bare area at lower left is vertical Paleozoic limestone surrounded on three sides by nearly horizontal rhyolite lava flows. Bare slope at lower right is west-dipping Pinyon Conglomerate, also overlapped by lava. Grand Teton is on right skyline and Mt. Moran is rounded summit on middle skyline.*

another. For example, the middle Eocene rocks are white to light-green, red, and purple, upper Eocene are dark-green, Oligocene are light-gray, white, and brown, Miocene are dark-green, brown, and gray, and Pliocene are white to red-brown.

As mentioned earlier, it is probable that the vast outpouring of volcanic rocks during late Tertiary time in the Teton region and to the north and northeast is directly related to the subsidence of Jackson Hole and the rise of the Tetons.

The spectacular banded cliffs of the Wiggins Formation on both sides of Togwotee Pass (fig. 52) and farther north in the Absaroka Range are remnants of Oligocene volcanic conglomerate and tuff that once spread as a blanket

Figure 54. *Obsidian, a volcanic glass less than 10 million years old, especially prized by Indians who used it for spear and arrow points and for tools.*

several thousand feet thick across eastern Jackson Hole and partially or completely buried the nearby older folded mountain ranges.

About 25 million years ago, with the start of the Miocene Epoch, volcanic vents opened up within, and along the borders of, Grand Teton National Park. Major centers of eruption were at the north end of the Teton Range, east of Jackson Lake, and south of Spread Creek. They emitted a prodigious amount of volcanic ash and fragments of congealed lava. For example, adjacent to one vent a mile in diameter, about 4 miles north-northeast of Jackson Lake Lodge, is a continuous section, 7,000 feet thick, of water-laid strata derived in large part from this volcanic source. These sedimentary rocks comprise the Colter Formation which is darker colored and contains more iron and magnesium than the Wiggins Formation. The site of deposition at this locality was a north-trending trough that represented an early stage in the downwarping of Jackson Hole.

Pliocene volcanoes erupted in southern and central Yellowstone Park. The volcanoes emitted viscous, frothy, pinkish-gray and brown lava called *rhyolite*. This is an extrusive igneous rock that has the same composition

100

Figure 55. *East face of Signal Mountain showing Bivouac Formation (upper Pliocene or Pleistocene). Tilted ledge is rhyolitic welded tuff 2.5 million years old, and slopes above and below it are conglomerate. National Park Service photo by W. E. Dilley.*

as granite, but is much finer grained. In several places, lava apparently flowed into the north end of Teewinot Lake, chilled suddenly, and solidified into a black volcanic glass called *obsidian*. Because it chips easily into thin flakes having a smooth surface, obsidian was prized by the Indians, who used it for spear and arrow points (fig. 54). Some of this obsidian has a potassium-argon date of 9 million years.

After Teewinot Lake was filled with sediment, the floor of Jackson Hole became a flat boulder-covered surface. Nearby vents erupted heavy fiery clouds of gaseous molten rock that rolled across this plain and then congealed into hard layers with the general appearance of lava flows. Under a microscope, however, the rock is seen to be made up of compressed fragments of glass that matted down and solidified when the clouds stopped moving. This kind of rock is called a *welded tuff*. One of these forms the conspicuous ledge in the Bivouac Formation on the north and east sides of Signal Mountain (fig. 55), and is especially important because it has a potassium-argon date of 2.5 million years. More of this welded tuff flowed southward from Yellowstone National Park, engulfed the north end of the Teton Range (fig. 53), and continued southward along the west side of the mountains for 35 miles and along the east side for 25 miles.

101

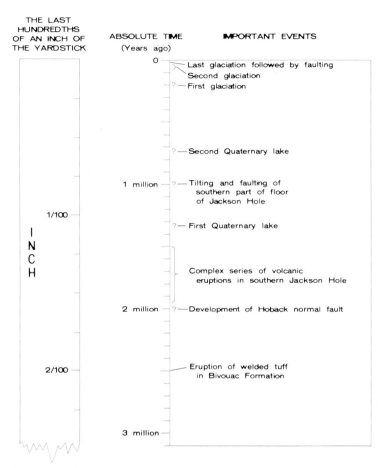

Figure 56. *The final 3 million years on our yardstick of time, enlarged to show approximate dates of major events.*

QUATERNARY-TIME OF ICE, MORE LAKES, AND CONTINUED CRUSTAL DISTURBANCE

The Quaternary Period is represented by less than 15-thousandths of the last inch on our yardstick of time (fig. 56) and the entire Ice Age takes up less than 2-thousandths of an inch (less than the thickness of this page). Nevertheless, the spectacular effects of various forces of nature on the Teton landscape during this short interval of time are of such significance that they warrant a separate discussion.

102

The role of glaciers in carving the rugged Teton peaks and shaping the adjacent valleys was mentioned in the first part of this booklet, but is discussed in more detail here. The magnitude and complexity of crustal movements increased during the final 2 million years of time—so much so that the beginning of Quaternary time has not yet been identified with any single event. Figure 56 shows the major events described below.

Hoback normal fault

The *Hoback normal fault*, 30 miles long, with a mile or more displacement, developed in the southernmost part of Jackson Hole about 2 million years ago. This fault is on the east side of the valley. Thus, the valley block was down-dropped between this fault and the Teton fault that borders the west side.

Volcanic activity

During or shortly after major movement on the Hoback fault, and perhaps related to it, there was a complex series of volcanic eruptions west and north of the town of Jackson, along the south boundary of the park. In rapid succession, lavas of many types, with a combined thickness of more than 1,000 feet, were extruded and volcanic plugs intruded into the near-surface sedimentary rocks. These volcanic rocks can be seen on the East and West Gros Ventre Buttes.

There are no active volcanoes in the Teton region today and no postglacial lava flows or cinder cones. Five miles north of Grand Teton National Park are boiling springs (Flagg Ranch hot springs) that are associated with the youngest (late Quaternary) lavas in southern Yellowstone Park. Elsewhere in Jackson Hole are a number of luke-warm springs but their relation to volcanic rocks has not been determined.

What happened to the vast thicknesses of volcanic debris? We know they existed because sections of them have been measured on the eroded edges of uptilted folds and fault blocks. Many cubic miles of these rocks are now buried beneath the floor of Jackson Hole, but a much greater volume was carried completely out of the region by water, ice, and wind during the final chapter of geologic history.

Remnants of two sets of lake deposits in Jackson Hole record preglacial events in Quaternary time. Downdropping of southern Jackson Hole along the Hoback and Teton faults blocked the southwestward drainage of the Snake River, and a new lake formed overlapping and extending south of the site of the long-vanished Teewinot Lake. Incorporated in the lake sediments are fragments of lava like that in nearby Quaternary flows. From this we know that the lake formed after at least some of the lava was emplaced. Apparently subsidence was more rapid than filling, for a time, at least, because this new lake was deep. Fossil snails preserved in olive-drab to gray fine-grained claystone overlying lava flows at the north end of East Gros Ventre Butte are the kind now living at depths of 120 to 300 feet in Lake Tahoe, California-Nevada. Near the margins of the lake, pink and green claystone and soft sandstone were deposited. The duration of this lake is not known but it lasted long enough for 200 feet of beds to accumulate. Subsequent faulting and warping destroyed the lake, left tilted remnants of the beds perched 1,000 feet up on the east side of Jackson Hole, and permitted the Snake River to reestablish its course across the mountains to the southwest.

Later downdropping of Jackson Hole impounded a second preglacial lake. Little is known about its extent because nearly everywhere the soft brown and gray shale, claystone, and sandstone deposited in it were scooped out and washed away during subsequent glaciations. A few remnants of the lake deposits are preserved in protected places, however; two are within the Gros Ventre River Valley—one downstream from Lower Slide Lake about a mile east of the park and the other 4 miles farther east. The latter remnant is nearly 500 feet thick and the upper half is largely very fine grained shale and claystone. This fine texture suggests that the lake existed for a good many thousand years, for such deposits commonly accumulate more slowly than coarser grained debris.

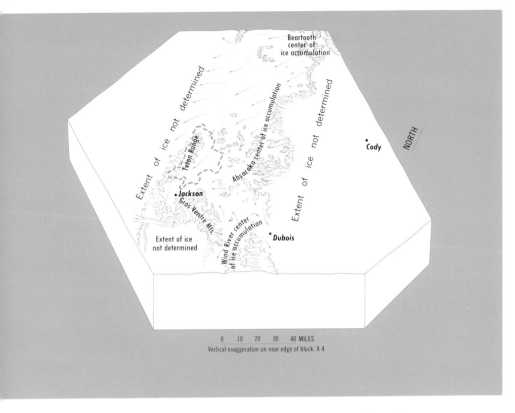

Figure 57. *Map showing extent and direction of movement of first and largest ice sheet. See figure 41 for State lines and location map.*

The Ice Age

With the uplift of the Teton Range and the formation of Jackson Hole late in Cenozoic time the landscape gradually began to assume the general outlines that we see today. Rain, wind, snow, and frost shaped the first crude approximations of the present ridges and peaks. Streams cut into the rising Teton fault block, eroding the ancestral canyons deeper and deeper as the uplift continued. The most recent great chapter in the story of the Teton landscape, however, remained to be written by the glaciers of the *Ice Age.*

The reasons for the climatic changes that caused the Ice Age are still a matter of much scientific debate. Various theories have been advanced that attribute them to changes in solar radiation, changes in the earth's orbit and inclination to the sun, variations in the amount of carbon dioxide in the atmosphere, shifts in the positions of the continents or the poles, and to many other factors, but none has met with universal acceptance. No doubt the explanation lies in some unusual combination of circumstances, for widespread glaciation occurred only twice before in the earth's history—once in the late Precambrian and once during the Permian. It is quite clear, however, that the glaciers did not form in response to any local cause such as the uplift of the Teton Range, for concurrent climatic changes and ice advance took place throughout many parts of the world.

At least three times in the last 250,000 years glaciers from the surrounding highlands invaded Jackson Hole. The oldest and most widespread glaciation probably took place about 200,000 years ago; it was called the *Buffalo Glaciation* by Prof. Eliot Blackwelder in 1915 (see selected references). The age estimate is based on measurements of the thickness of the decomposed layer on the surface of obsidian pebbles in the glacial debris. Major sources of ice were the Beartooth Mountains (fig. 1), the Absaroka Range, and the Wind River Range. The Gros Ventre Mountains and Teton Range furnished lesser amounts of ice.

The ice from the Beartooth and Absaroka centers of ice accumulation converged in the northeastern part of Grand Teton National Park and flowed south along the face of the Teton Range in a giant stream that in many places was 2,000 feet thick (fig. 57). All but the highest parts of the Pinyon Peak and Mount Leidy Highlands were buried and scoured. Signal Mountain, Blacktail Butte, and the Gros Ventres Buttes were overridden and shaped by ice at this time. Another glacier, this one from the Wind River Range, flowed northwest along the Continental Divide, then down the Gros Ventre River Valley, and merged with the southward-moving main ice stream west of Lower Slide Lake. Where Jackson Hole narrows southward, the glacier became more and more confined, but nevertheless flowed all the way through the Snake River Canyon and on into Idaho.

The volume of this great ice mass was probably con-

Figure 58. *Glacial deposits, outwash, and loess exposed along Boyle Ditch in Jackson Hole National Elk Refuge. Indicated are middle Pliocene Teewinot Formation (A), oldest till (B), Bull Lake outwash gravel (C), and post-Bull Lake loess (D), which here contains snail shells dated by Carbon-14 as 15,000 years old. Height of cliff is about 30 feet.*

siderably more than 1,000 cubic miles. When it melted, nearly all the previously accumulated soil in Jackson Hole was washed away and a pavement of quartzite boulders mantled much of the glaciated surface. In areas not subsequently glaciated, the lack of soil and abundance of quartzite boulders drastically influenced the topography, later drainage, distribution of all types of vegetation, especially conifers and grass, and the pattern of human settlement and industry.

Figure 59. *View west from the Snake River overlook showing at upper right the Burned Ridge moraine (with trees) merging southward with the highest (oldest) Pinedale outwash plain. The next lower surface is composed of outwash from the Jackson Lake moraine which lies to the right, out of the picture. At the bottom is Deadman's Bar, a gravel deposit at the present river level. Photo by H. D. Pownall.*

The second glaciation, named *Bull Lake,* was less than half as extensive as the first. A large tongue of ice from the Absaroka center of accumulation flowed down the Buffalo River Valley and joined ice from the Tetons on the floor of Jackson Hole. An enormous outwash fan of quartzite boulders extended from near Blacktail Butte southward throughout most of southern Jackson Hole. Glaciers in the Gros Ventre Mountains did not advance beyond the east margin of the valley floor. Carbon-14 ages and data from weathered obsidian pebbles suggest that this glaciation took place between 35,000 and 80,000 years ago.

Bull Lake moraines and outwash deposits are overlain directly in the southern part of Jackson Hole by fine silt, rather than by deposits of the third glaciation (fig. 58). This silt, of windblown origin, is called *loess* and contains

Figure 60. *Air oblique view west toward the Teton Range, showing effects of Pinedale Glaciation on the landscape. Mt. Moran is at top left; the mountain front is broken by U-shaped valleys from which ice emerged into the area now occupied by Jackson Lake. The timbered area bordering Jackson Lake is the Jackson Lake moraine. One of the braided outlet channels breaching the Jackson Lake moraine can be seen crossing the outwash plain at the left center. Lakes at lower right occupy "potholes" near where the 9,000-year-old snail shells occur. Snake River is in foreground. Photo by R. L. Casebeer.*

fossil shells dated by Carbon-14 as between 13,000 and 19,000 years old. Wherever the loess occurs, it is marked by abundant modern coyote dens and badger burrows.

The third and last glaciation, named the *Pinedale,* was even less extensive than the others. Nevertheless it was of great importance for it added the final touches to the present landscape. The jagged intricately ice-carved peaks (fig. 4) and the glittering lakes and broad gravelly plains are vivid reminders of this recent chapter in geologic history.

Pinedale glaciers advanced down Cascade, Garnet, Avalanche, and Death Canyons and spilled out onto the floor of Jackson Hole, where they built the outermost loops of the conspicuous terminal moraines that now encircle Jenny, Bradley, Taggart, and Phelps Lakes (fig. 13). Ice streams from Glacier Gulch and Open Canyon also left

109

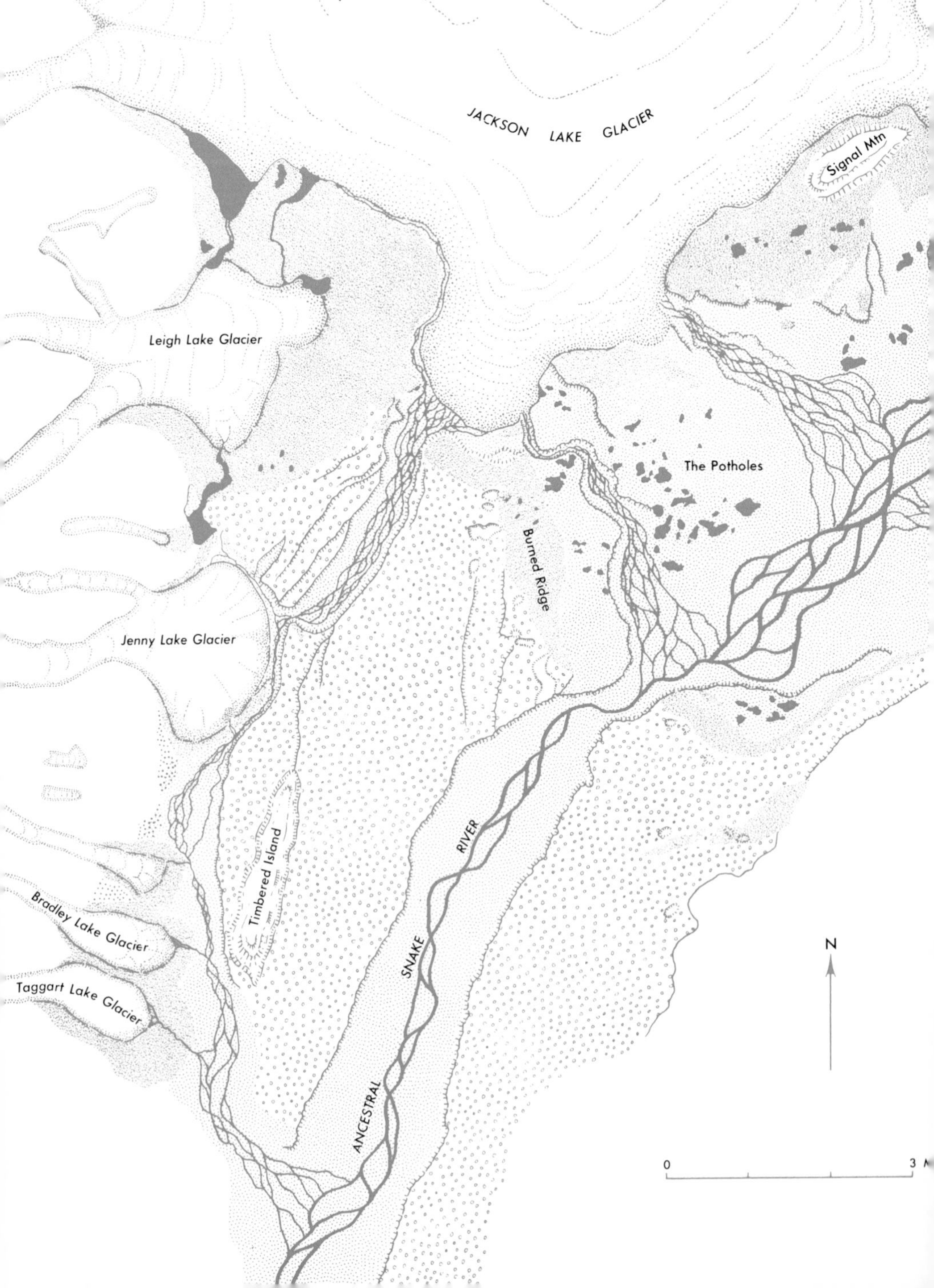

Figure 61. *The Pinedale Glaciers in the central part of Jackson Hole as they might have appeared at the time the Jackson Lake moraine was built. Solid color areas are lakes; dark irregular pattern shows areas of moraine deposited during the maximum advance of the Pinedale Glaciers. Pattern of open circles shows older Pinedale outwash plains; pattern of fine dots shows outwash plains built at the time the glaciers were in the positions shown in the drawing. Coarser dots near the margins of the glaciers represent concentrations of rock debris in the ice.*

prominent moraines on the valley floor, but these do not contain lakes. Ice from Leigh Canyon and all of the eastward-draining valleys to the north combined to form a large glacier in roughly the present position of Jackson Lake. This ice entirely surrounded Signal Mountain, leaving only the upper few hundred feet projecting as an island or *nunatak*.

The southernmost major advance of Pinedale ice from Jackson Lake is marked by a series of densely timbered moraines that cross the Snake River Valley. This series is collectively named the *Burned Ridge moraine* (fig. 61). Extending southward for 10 miles from this moraine is a remarkably flat surfaced gravelly outwash deposit. It was spread by streams that poured from the glacier at the time the moraine was being built (fig. 59). East of the Snake River, the main highway from a point just north of Blacktail Butte to the Snake River overlook is built on this flat untimbered surface. We assume that the outwash is younger than 15,000 years because it apparently overlies loess of that age.

The glacier withdrew rapidly northward from the Burned Ridge moraine, leaving behind many large irregular masses of stagnant, debris-covered ice. The sites of these became kettles, locally known as "The Potholes" (fig. 12). The main glacier retreated to a position marked by the loop of moraines just south of Jackson Lake (fig. 60). Figure 61 is a sketch map showing how the glaciers in this part of Jackson Hole might have appeared at the time the Jackson Lake moraine was built.

Abundant snail shells have been found in lake sediments in the bottoms of the kettles north of the Burned Ridge moraine (fig. 60) as well as on low ridges between them. Carbon-14 age determinations indicate that the snails lived about 9,000 years ago, either in a lake already present before the Pinedale ice advanced and formed the Burned Ridge moraine or in ponds that filled kettles left as the ice melted behind this moraine.

In either case, the shells indicate that the Pinedale glaciers probably existed on the floor of Jackson Hole as recently as 9,000 years ago, at a time when Indians were already living in the area. We can easily imagine the fascination with which these primitive peoples may have watched as year after year the glaciers wasted away, slowly retreating back into the canyons, then withdrawing into the sheltered recesses of the high mountains, eventually to dwindle and disappear.

Many bits of evidence, both from North America and Europe, indicate that there was a period called the *climatic optimum* about 6,000 years ago when the climate was significantly warmer and drier than at present. We suspect, though there is as yet no direct proof, that the Pinedale glaciers wasted away entirely during this interval.

The modern pattern of vegetation in Jackson Hole is strongly influenced by the distribution of Pinedale glacial moraines and outwash deposits. Almost without exception the moraines are heavily forested, whereas the nearby outwash deposits are covered only by a sparse growth of sagebrush. This is probably because the moraines contain large amounts of clay and silt produced by the grinding action of the glaciers. Material of this type retains water much better and, because of the greater variety of chemical elements, is more fertile than the porous quartzite gravel and sand on the outwash plains.

Modern glaciers

About a dozen small rapidly dwindling glaciers exist today in shaded reentrants high in the Teton Range. They are probably vestiges of ice masses built up since the climatic optimum, during the so-called *"Little Ice Age."* These glaciers, while insignificant compared to those still present in many other mountain ranges, are fascinating working models of the great ice streams that shaped the Tetons during Pleistocene time.

The Teton Glacier (fig. 6) is one of the best known. It is an ice body about 3,500 feet long and 1,100 feet wide that lies at the head of Glacier Gulch, shaded by the encircling ridges of the Grand Teton, Mount Owen, and Mount Teewinot. Ice in the central part is moving at a rate of more than 30 feet a year.

THE PRESENT AND THE FUTURE

The geologic story of the Teton country from the time the earth was new to the present day has been summarized. What can we learn from it? We become aware that events recorded in the rocks are not a chaotic jumble of random accidents but came in an orderly, logical succession. We see the majestic parade of life evolving from simple to complex types, overcoming all natural disasters, and adapting to ever-changing environments. We can only speculate as to the motivating force that launched this fascinating geologic and biologic venture and what the ultimate goal may be. New facts and new ideas are added to the story each year, but many unknown chapters remain to be studied; these offer an irresistible, continuing challenge to inquisitive minds, strong bodies, and restless, adventurous spirits.

Most geologic processes that developed the Teton landscape have been beneficial to man; a few have interfered with his activities, cost him money, time, effort, and on occasion, his life. Postglacial faulting and tilting along the southern margin of Grand Teton National Park diverted drainage systems (such as Flat Creek, southwest of the Flat Creek fault on the south edge of the geologic map), raised hills, dropped valleys, and made steep slopes unstable. Flood-control engineers wage a never-ending struggle to keep the Snake River from shifting to the west side of Jackson Hole as the valley tilts westward in response to movement along the Teton fault. Each highway into Jackson Hole has been blocked by a landslide at one time or another and maintenance of roads across slide areas requires much ingenuity. We see one slide (the Gros Ventre) that blocked a river; larger slides have occurred in the past, and more can be expected. Abundant fresh fault scarps are a constant reminder that public buildings, campgrounds, dams, and roads need to be designed to withstand the effects of earthquakes. Some of these problems have geologic solutions; others can be avoided or minimized as further study increases our understanding of this region.

Man appeared during the last one-fiftieth of an inch on our yardstick of time gone by. In this short span he has had more impact on the earth and its inhabitants than any other form of life. Will he use wisely the lessons of the past as a guide while he writes his record on the yardstick of the future?

APPENDIX
Acknowledgements

This booklet could not have been prepared without the cooperation and assistance of many individuals and organizations. We are indebted to the National Park Service for the use of facilities, equipment, and photographs, and for the enthusiasm and interest of all of the park staff. We especially appreciate the cooperation, advice, and assistance rendered by the late Fred C. Fagergren, former superintendent of Grand Teton National Park; Willard E. Dilley, former chief park naturalist; and R. Alan Mebane, former assistant chief park naturalist.

Profs. Charles C. Bradley and John Montagne of Montana State University and Bruno J. Giletti of Brown University generously provided us with unpublished data. Cooperators during the years of background research were the late Dr. H. D. Thomas, State Geologist of Wyoming, and Dr. D. L. Blackstone, Jr., Chairman, Department of Geology, University of Wyoming.

Helpful suggestions were made by many of our colleagues with the U. S. Geological Survey; S. S. Oriel, in particular, gave unstintingly of his time and talents in the review and revision of an early version of the manuscript. A later version had the further benefit of critical review by three other people, all experienced in presenting various types of scientific data to public groups: John M. Good, former chief park naturalist of Yellowstone National Park; Bryan Harry, former assistant chief park naturalist of Grand Teton National Park; and Richard Klinck, "1965 National Teacher of the Year."

We are indebted to Ann C. Christiansen, Geologic Map Editor, for advice and guidance on the illustrations and to R. C. Fuhrmann and his staff for preparation of many of the line drawings. Block diagrams and photo artwork were prepared by J. R. Stacy and R. A. Reilly. All photographs without specific credit lines are by the authors. From the beginning of the Teton field study to editing and proofing of the final manuscript, our wives, Jane M. Love and Linda H. Reed, have been enthusiastic and indispensable participants.

Blackwelder, Eliot, 1915, Post-Cretaceous history of the mountains of central western Wyoming: Jour. Geology, v. 23, p. 97-117, 193-217, 307-340.

Bradley, F. H., 1873, Report on the geology of the Snake River district: U.S. Geol. Survey Terr. 6th Ann. Rept. (Hayden), p. 190-271.

Edmund, R. W., 1951, Structural geology and physiography of the northern end of the Teton Range, Wyoming: Augustana Library Pub. 23, 82 p.

Fryxell, F. M., 1930, Glacial features of Jackson Hole, Wyoming: Augustana Library Pub. 13, 129 p.

_____, 1938, The Tetons, interpretations of a mountain landscape: Univ. California Press, Berkeley, Calif., 77 p.

Hague, Arnold, 1904, Atlas to accompany U.S. Geol. Survey Monograph 32 on the geology of Yellowstone National Park.

_____, Iddings, J. P., Weed, W. H., and others, 1899 Geology of the Yellowstone National Park: U.S. Geol. Survey Monograph 32, Pt. 2, 893 p.

Harry, Bryan, 1963, Teton trails, a guide to the trails of Grand Teton National Park: Grand Teton Natural History Association, Moose, Wyo., 56 p.

Horberg, Leland, 1938, The structural geology and physiography of the Teton Pass area, Wyoming: Augustana Library Pub. 16, 86 p.

Hurley, P. M., 1959, How old is the earth?: Anchor Books, Garden City, N. Y., 160 p.

Ortenburger, Leigh, 1965, A climber's guide to the Teton Range: Sierra Club, San Francisco, 336 p.

St. John, O. H., 1883, Report on the geology of the Wind River district: U.S. Geol. Geog. Survey Terr. 12th Ann. Rept. (Hayden), Pt. 1, p. 173-270.

Wyoming Geological Association, 1956, Guidebook, 11th annual field conf., Jackson Hole, Wyoming, 1956, Casper, Wyo., 256 p., incl. sketch maps, diagrams, tables, and illus., also geol. map, sections, and charts. Composed of a series of individual papers by various authors.

J. D. Love, a native of Wyoming, received his bachelor and master of arts degrees from the University of Wyoming and his doctor of philosophy degree from Yale University. His first field season in the Teton country, in 1933, was financed by the Geological Survey of Wyoming. After 12 years of geologic work ranging from New England to Utah and Michigan to Mississippi, he returned to the Teton region. Beginning in 1945, he spent parts or all of 20 field seasons in and near the Tetons. He compiled the first geologic map of Teton County. He is the senior author of the geologic map of Wyoming, and author or co-author of more than 70 other published maps and papers on the geology of Wyoming. In 1961, the University of Wyoming awarded him an honorary doctor of laws degree for his work on uranium deposits that "led to the development of the uranium industry in Wyoming." The Wyoming Geological Association made him an honorary life member and gave him a special award for his geologic studies of the Teton area. He is a Fellow of the Geological Society of America and is active in various other geological organizations, as well as having been president of the Wyoming Chapters of Sigma Xi (scientific honorary) and Phi Beta Kappa (scholastic honorary) societies.

John C. Reed, Jr., joined the U.S. Geological Survey in 1953 after receiving his doctor of philosophy degree from the John Hopkins University. His principal geologic work before coming to the Teton region was in Alaska and in the southern Appalachians. Beginning in 1961, he spent five field seasons studying and mapping the Precambrian rocks in Grand Teton National Park, including all the high peaks in the Teton Range. He is a noted mountaineer, a Fellow of the Geological Society of America, a member of the Arctic Institute of North America, and the American Alpine Club. His numerous publications, in addition to those on the Tetons, describe the geology of mountainous areas in Alaska, the Appalachians, and Utah.

Index of selected terms and features

Term	Defined or described on page
amphibolite	51
anticlines	85
badlands	14
bentonite	81
biotite	51
brachiopods	70
Buffalo Glaciation	106
Bull Lake Glaciation	108
Burned Ridge moraine	111
buttes	18
Carbon-14	48
carnivores	95
chlorite	56
cirque	30
climatic optimum	162
Cordilleran trough	69
diabase	59
dikes	56
dipping	39
dolomite	75
"edgewise" conglomerate	73
epochs	46
eras	46
erosion	27
erratics	31
extrusive igneous rocks	46
fault	9
fault block mountain range	37
fault scarps	37
formations	66
frost wedging	25
geologic	10
glacial striae	30
gradients	28
Grand Valley Lake	95
granite	55
granite gneiss	54
groups	47
gypsum	79
herbivores	95
Hoback normal fault	103
hole	8
hornblende	51
Ice Age	105
igneous rocks	46
intrusive igneous rocks	46

Jackson Hole 8
jade 55

kettle 31

Laramide Revolution 82
lateral moraine 30
layered gneisses 51
Little Ice Age 112
loess 108

magma 60
magnetite 52
marine sedimentary rocks 21
metamorphic rocks 53
muscovite 55

normal fault 39
nunatak 111

obsidian 101
oreodonts 97
outwash 31
outwash plain 31
outwash terraces 34

pegmatite 56
period 46
Pinedale Glaciation 109

quartzite 63

reverse fault 39
rhyolite 100
rock glaciers 26

schist 51
sedimentary rocks 45
series 47
serpentine 55
"soapstone" 55
Sundance Sea 79
systems 46

talus 24
Targhee uplift 83
Teewinot Lake 92
Tetons 8
Teton fault 37
terminal moraine 30
thrust fault 39
timberline 15
titanothere 97
treeline 15
Triceratops 85
trilobites 70
tuff 92

welded tuff 101

**The
GRAND TETON
NATURAL HISTORY
ASSOCIATION**

The Grand Teton Natural History Association assists the National Park Service in the development of a broad public understanding of the geology, plant and animal life, history, and related subjects pertaining to Grand Teton National Park. It aids in the development of museums and wayside exhibits, offers for sale publications on natural and human history, and cooperates with the Government in the interest of Grand Teton National Park.

Mail orders: For a publication list, write the Grand Teton Natural History Association, Moose, Wyoming 83012.